A Trump Family Christmas

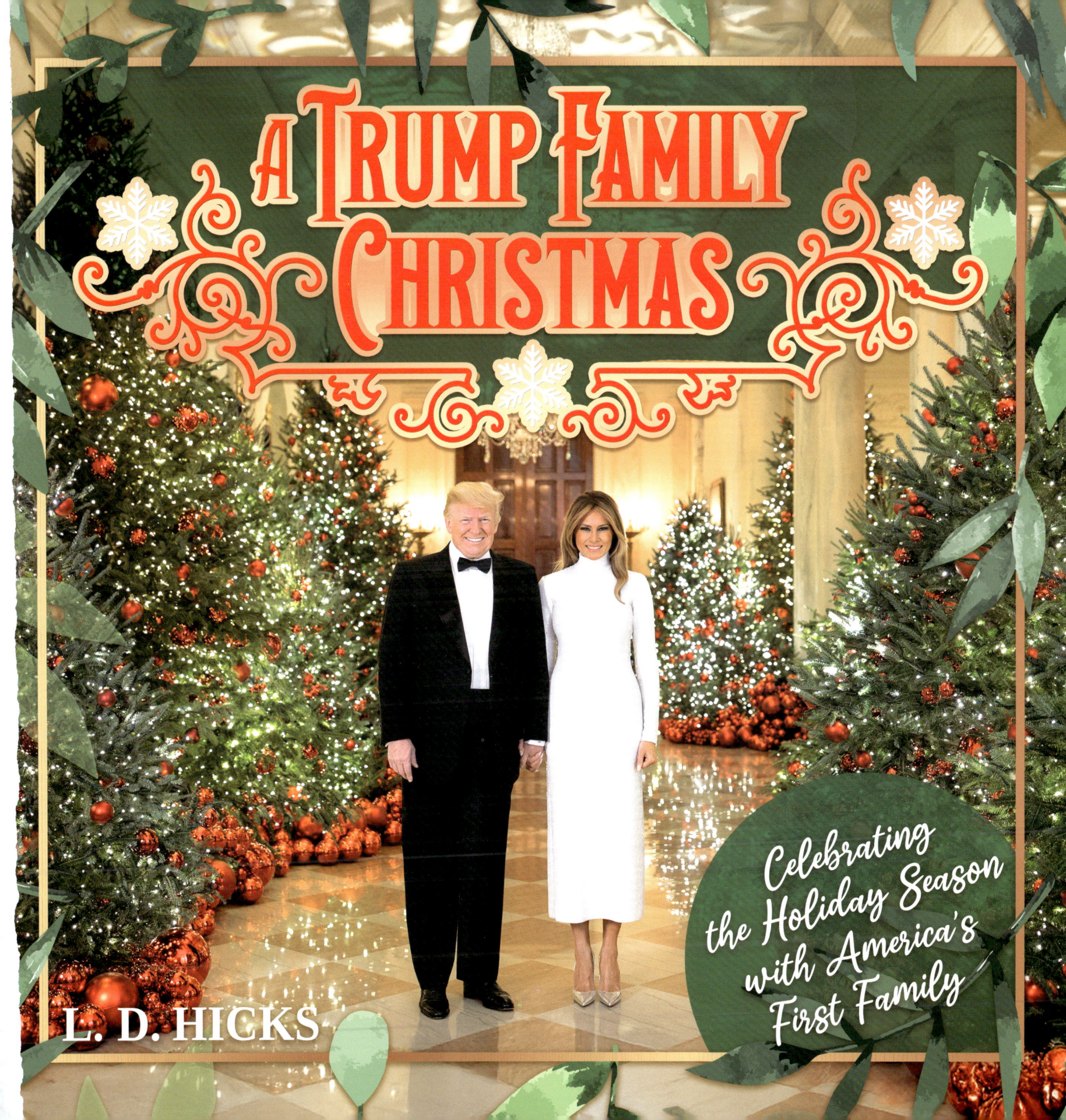

Celebrating the Holiday Season with America's First Family

L. D. HICKS

A Trump Family Christmas

L. D. HICKS

Post Hill
PRESS

A POST HILL PRESS BOOK
ISBN: 979-8-89565-249-7

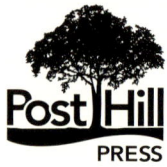

Post Hill Press
New York • Nashville
posthillpress.com

Published in the United States of America
1 2 3 4 5 6 7 8 9 10

Printed in Canada

A Tapestry of Love and Legacy

When President Donald J. Trump and Melania Knauss exchanged vows on January 22, 2005, at the Episcopal Church of Bethesda-by-the-Sea, in Palm Beach, Florida, they not only began a new chapter as husband and wife, but also embarked on the journey of blending traditions, cultures, and family legacies. Like many blended families today, it takes time to merge customs, weaving together a rich and beautiful tapestry of love and hope, beauty and history, community and heritage. Their union represented more than just their new marriage—it was a forging of new ties between two families, two communities, and two cultures that spanned continents and crossed the Atlantic Ocean.

The history of Christmas mirrors this fusion of tradition and culture. Many Americans do not know that the song "Silent Night" originated in Germany, or that before Santa Claus became an icon of the Coca Cola brand, he was revered as a German saint and an Austrian elf. In my own marriage, my family's Christmas tree had always been decorated with every ornament our family had collected over the years, while my wife's family had always celebrated a themed Christmas. Traditions like these came together to become new customs that our family as well as future generations would cherish and carry forward.

Donald's Family Upbringing

Donald Trump comes from a family of German immigrants. On October 7, 1885, his grandfather, Friedrich Trump, climbed aboard a ship with a one-way ticket to New York City. Arriving in the city that never sleeps, he took many different jobs to make a

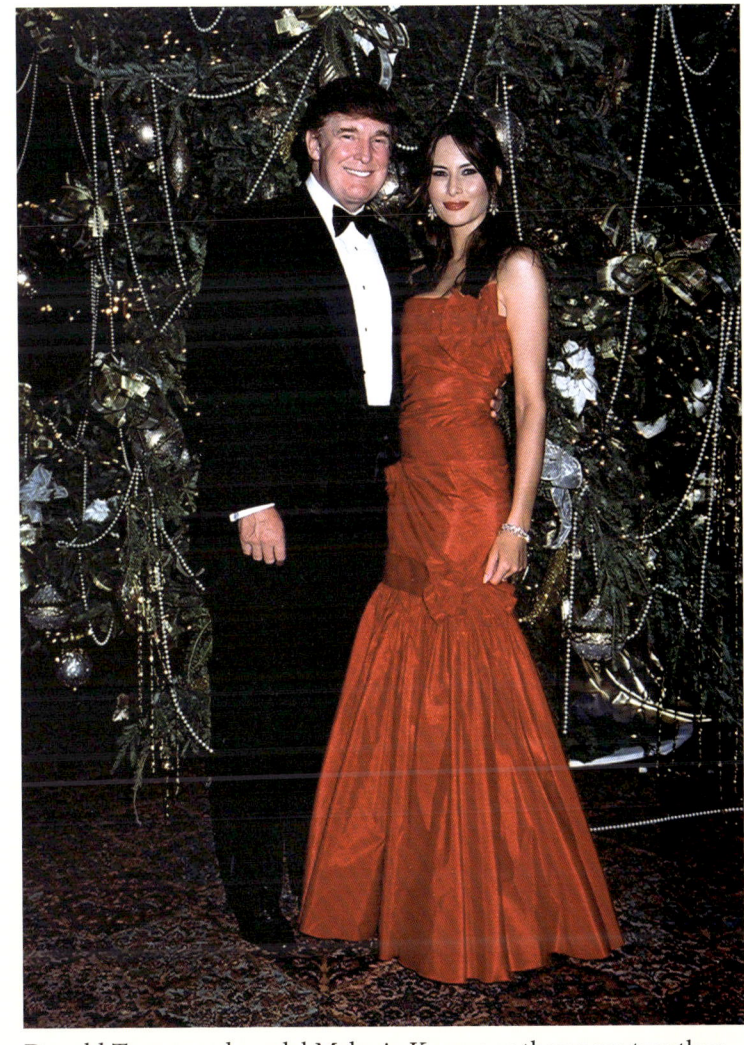

Donald Trump and model Melania Knauss as they pose together in front of a Christmas tree at the Mar-a-Lago estate, Palm Beach, Florida, 2002. (Photo by Davidoff Studios/Getty Images)

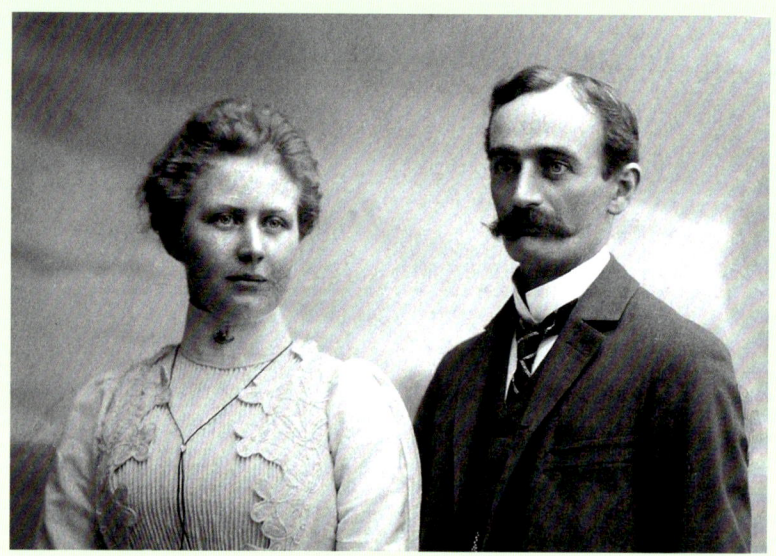

Friedrich Trump and Elizabeth Christ (Public Domain)

living, working as a bartender, a barber, a saloon-hotelier, and ultimately, a New York real estate investor. Eventually, he chased his dreams out west to Seattle, where he opened restaurants to serve the folks coming and going from the city and its ports to the gold fields and settlements. Through hard work, perseverance, and creativity, the Trump patriarch began the legacy that would eventually become the family's fortune.

Friedrich Trump sailed home to Germany, where he married a woman who had grown up across the street from him, Elizabeth Christ, and brought her back to NYC. Friedrich went back to barbering in the financial district, and while they were living in the Bronx, President Trump's father, Frederick, was born. Sadly, Friedrich Trump would pass away in the horrific influenza outbreak of 1918.

The Trumps would have brought their German Christmas traditions with them to the United States. The initials of the three wise men—Caspar, Melchior, and Balthasar—would be inscribed with chalk over doorways to keep a house and home safe. They would have sung *Stille Nacht,* or "Silent Night," which was originally written in German. Kris Kringle would have visited and given presents. In the German neighborhood the Trumps lived in, starting in November, there would have been Christmas fairs with warm drinks, chestnuts, and local crafts for sale. Many of the traditions we celebrate on Christmas originated in Germany.

After years of toil and enterprise, Friedrich left his family a large inheritance upon his death in 1918. Elizabeth Christ Trump carried on the family business, and their son Fred began building homes when he was seventeen. Fred had brilliant business acumen and was able to forecast where housing was needed and business would boom. Eventually he bought into grocery stores and mortgage companies and founded the great nest of the Trump fortune.

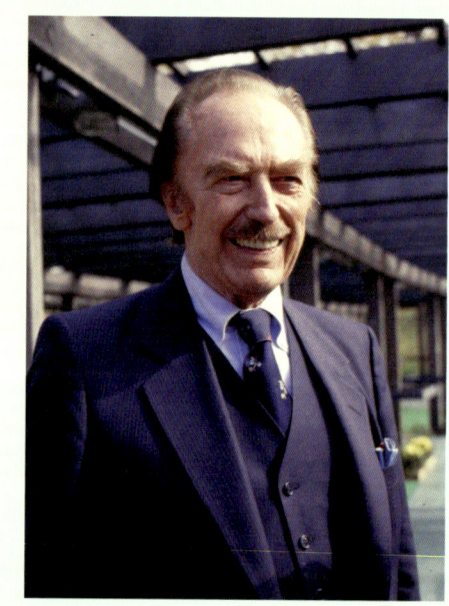

Fred Trump (Photo by Bernard Gotfryd, Public Domain)

In 1912, on the Isle of Lewis, in a tiny fishing village called Tong, Mary Anne MacLeod was born. She was the youngest of ten children and grew up speaking Gaelic, a Celtic language spoken in Scotland. English was her second language, taught to her in primary school. At the age of eighteen, with little prospects in the poor fishing village of Tong, she emigrated to the United States on a ship out of Glasgow, Scotland.

Mary arrived in New York City with fifty dollars in her purse, and worked hard as a domestic servant and a nanny. Sometime after she turned twenty-three years old, Mary's sister Catherine took her to a party where she met Fred Trump.

The two hit it off, and when Fred went home that night, he told his mother he had met the woman he was going to marry. The two were wed on January 11, 1936, at a Presbyterian church in Manhattan. The couple had a whirlwind honeymoon, and upon their return Fred went back to work building houses and apartments, including much of what is now the five boroughs of New York City.

**

In Scotland, Christmas was not a national holiday until 1958. Most Scots considered Christmas an English holiday early in the twentieth century. Mary Anne Trump would have seen her father off to work on Christmas day on the island of Tong. Scots celebrate a New Year's holiday called Hogmanay. *Hogmanay* is the Scots word for the last day of the old year. Celebrations can take place from New Year's Eve until the first or second of January. Folks exchange gifts and share food and drink. Mary Anne's family spoke Gaelic in the household and their celebrations were rooted in Scottish traditions such as the "first-foot," or *ciad-chuairt*. The first-foot, the first person to enter the home on New Year's Day, was seen as a bringer of good fortune for the coming year. Mary Anne Trump would have brought this tradition into her new household with her new husband.

On June 14, 1946, Fred and Mary Anne Trump's fourth child, Donald J. Trump, was born. As President Trump grew to adulthood, he watched his father build a real estate domain that dominated the city of New York from Manhattan to the Bronx. Fred's determination and fierce work ethic were passed down to his son, who would expand and grow his father's business into a multibillion-dollar empire that spanned the world. Donald Trump's business savvy and talent for the art of making deals would catapult him all the way to the presidency and the history books of the United States.

Melania's Family Upbringing

On July 9, 1945, Amalija Ulcnik was born in Judendorf-Strassengel, Austria. Her family, like millions of others, had been displaced in the horror and aftermath of World War II. Amalija's father, Anton, a shoemaker and avid farmer, worked hard to provide for his family, doing whatever he could to help them survive. Upon moving back to the village of Raka, he bred a new vegetable, the Raka onion. Soon this vegetable would become renowned in the country of Slovenia and eventually become a staple for building flavors all over the world.

Followed in her father's creative footsteps, Amalija became an innovator in tailoring and creating clothing patterns. Unflagging in her endeavors, she was hired as a designer at a children's clothing factory in Sevnica. Amalija was a believer in taking care of yourself as well as others.

Viktor Knavs was born on November 23, 1941, in Radeče, Slovenia. During his youth, he fell in love with cars and motorcycles. Like many Americans of his generation who loved tuning and working on engines, Viktor became an expert in repairing and souping up cars. This hobby served him well in the Yugoslavian army, where he drove all sorts of equipment and was promoted to driving VIPS.

Viktor Knavs and Amalija Ulcnik met in Sevnica, Slovenia, in 1966, where he was a rising executive in the automobile industry

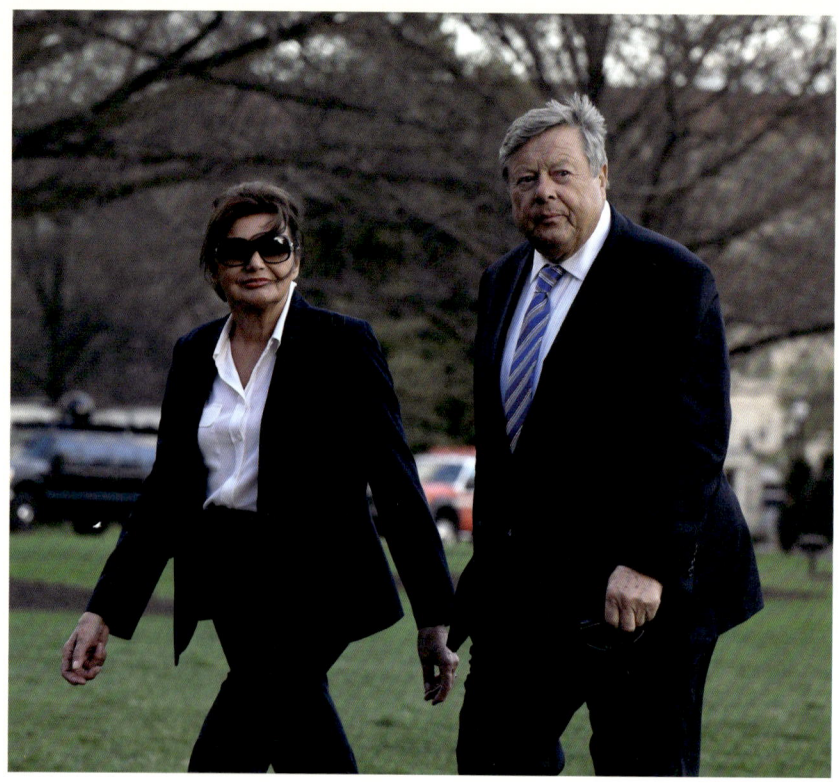

First lady Melania Trump's parents, Viktor Knavs and Amalija Knavs (Photo by Olivier Douliery/AFP via Getty Images)

and she was designing patterns for the local children's clothing manufacturer. They were married by the courts, but Amalija, a woman of faith, wanted a Catholic ceremony, something that was frowned upon underneath the Iron Curtain during the Cold War. Later on and in secret, they renewed their vows in St. Lawrence Church in Amalija's hometown in Austria. The couple began to rise in their professions despite living under a Communist regime that stifled creativity and drive in millions of people. With a strong work ethic passed down to them by their parents, each of them became successful despite the trauma of the post–World War II era and Tito's iron grip on Yugoslavia.

Viktor and Amalija's roots were in the mountainous country of Austria. Despite the disaster of World War II and the oppression of Communism, the rich Christmas tradition of the country would have been passed down to Viktor and Amalija. Folks attended Mass and cooked large meals to celebrate. Christmas trees were adorned with lights and decorations representing events in history or family lore. Advent wreaths made of evergreen branches were crisscrossed with ribbons and ornaments and placed on doors and walls. The star of Christmas dinner was fish rather than turkey, and it was often accompanied by dumplings, red cabbage, and potatoes.

Windows were left open at bedtime to allow the Christkind to deliver presents. Mothers baked vanilla crescent cookies and left out marzipan with mulled wine, just as we might leave milk and cookies for Santa and carrots for the reindeer. Folks would go ice skating, and carolers went from door to door singing. "Silent Night" would have been sung just like it is today.

On April 26, 1970, Amalija gave birth to her second daughter, Melanija, in Novo Mesto, Slovenia. Melania and her sister, Ines, were secretly baptized in the Catholic Church to avoid the strict rules of the Communists. As Melanija grew up, she was exposed to the hard work ethic of her parents as well as the allure of the fashion industry. She often modeled the children's clothing that her mother designed at various fashion shows. Melanija began developing and sewing her own clothing under the tutelage of her mother. After modeling in a teen fashion show at age sixteen, Melanija was discovered by a modeling scout. She changed the spelling of her name to Melania Knauss. The young model's work ethic, learned from her parents, served her well as her career took her to dizzying heights—Milan, Paris, and finally the United States. While working as a model in Manhattan in 1998, she was introduced to Donald Trump.

Bringing the Family Together

When Donald Trump and Melania Knauss were united in matrimony in Florida, each of their families' histories and cultural traditions were joined together as well—German, Austrian, Scottish, and Slovenian, not to mention the traditions they had each developed in their own adult lives. On March 20, 2006, their son, Barron Trump, was born in a Manhattan hospital. Ultimately, Barron is the recipient of all these cultures coming together for Christmas, at least until he has a family of his own.

Melania quickly fell into Christmas traditions within the blended Trump family. Christmas would be celebrated at Mar-a-Lago, Donald Trump's estate in Palm Beach, Florida, with an open invitation for all of President Trump's five children: Don Jr., Ivanka, Eric, Tiffany, and Barron. The Trumps attend Midnight Mass and Christmas Eve services at the church they were married in, the Church of Bethesda-by-the-Sea, the oldest church in Palm Beach. From the be-

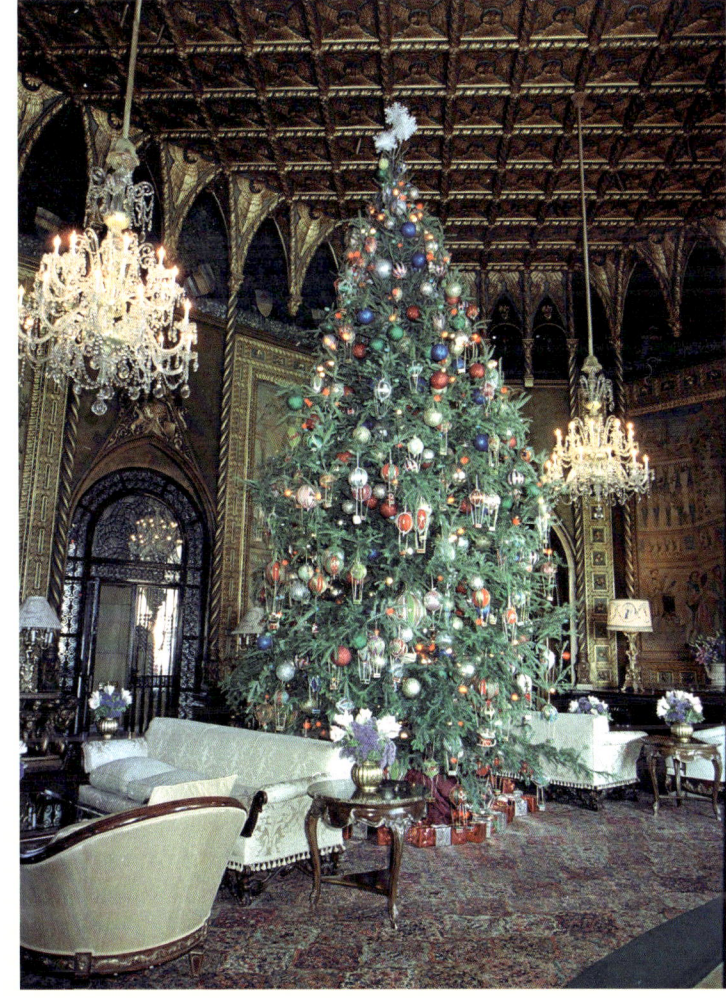

View of a Christmas tree in the main living room of the Mar-a-Lago club, Palm Beach, Florida, December 9, 2000. (Photo by Davidoff Studios/Getty Images)

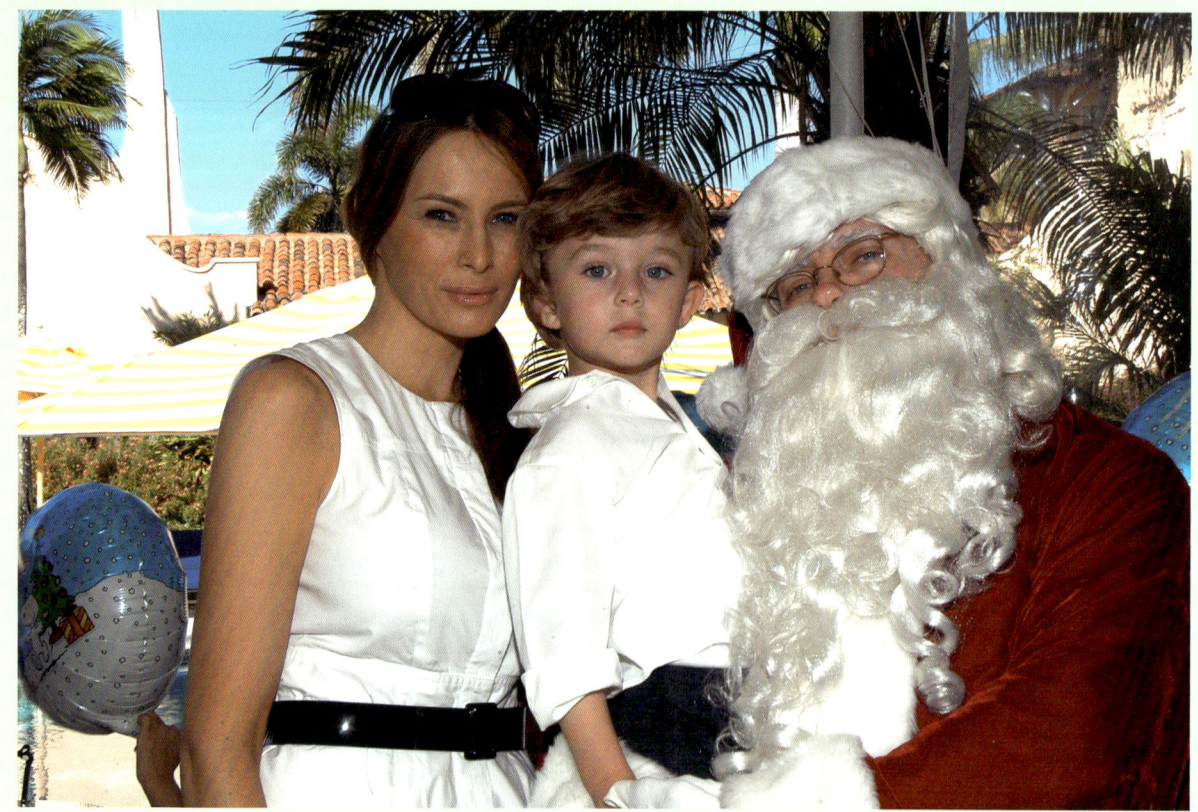

Melania Trump, Barron Trump, and Santa Claus on Christmas Day at the Mar-a-Lago estate in Palm Beach, Florida, December 25, 2008. (Photo by Davidoff Studios/Getty Images)

ginning, Melania ensured Mar-a-Lago was open to the whole family. Even President Trump's former wife Ivana spent Christmas there prior to her death. Before Mar-a-Lago became the go to Christmas destination, Don Jr. has spoken about spending Christmases with his father in the Trump Tower, the children running to jump into bed with their parents on Christmas morning before exchanging gifts. Barron's Christmas memories would have been no different.

Since the beginning of their marriage, Melania has made sure that family is the focal point of every Trump family holiday. Barron would have basked in the glow of not only his mother and father's love but would have been surrounded by his older half brothers and sisters, along with his many cousins. President Trump, Melania, and Barron spend Christmas like most Americans, surrounded by family and friends…with just a few *tiny* details most Americans do not have—like Air Force One to deliver family to Christmas dinner!

Just like their forebears, the Trumps enjoy a delicious feast on Christmas. In 2017, Christmas dinner featured President Trump's favorite wedge salad, followed by a decadent spread of turkey, filet mignon, foie gras, braised short ribs, pan-seared sea bass, and diver scallops. It was a meal worthy of a *Top Chef* finale—the kind of meal that makes a Christmas Day nap inevitable!

White House Traditions

Although the Trump family had all of their own traditions, when they became the First Family they also continued a lot of the traditions of previous White House residents. Christmas season at the White House kicks off with the receiving of the official White House Christmas tree. This tree is brought in via horse-drawn carriage and the First Lady is there to welcome it to the White House and meet the growers. According to the White House Historical Society, this tradition stretches all the way back to 1966 with Lady Bird Johnson. It's also up to the First Lady to pick a theme for the holiday decorations at the White House, a tradition which dates back to Jackie Kennedy in 1961. Every room of the White House is lovingly decorated with the help of volunteers from around the country. They travel far and wide to be a part of the holiday decorating tradition, and there are also performers who volunteer to perform at the holiday White House open houses throughout the season. There is also an official White House Gingerbread House that the pastry team at the White House puts a lot of time and effort into. These long honored traditions are the core of the holiday festivities at the White House and Melania beautifully took up the reins.

Outside of the decor and themes, the President and First Lady attend the National Tree Lighting Ceremony, answer phones for NORAD on Christmas Eve to talk to children about Santa sightings, and host many open houses at the White House throughout the holiday season. There are also many White House traditions centered around giving back to others. The First Lady visits with children and their families at Children's National hospital in Washington, DC, a tradition which dates back over 70 years to Bess Truman. She also attends events for Toys for Tots, spending some time giving back to military families who already give so much. The President will also take time to bring cheer to US service men and women overseas who cannot be home for Christmas with their families, with phone or video calls on Christmas Eve or Christmas

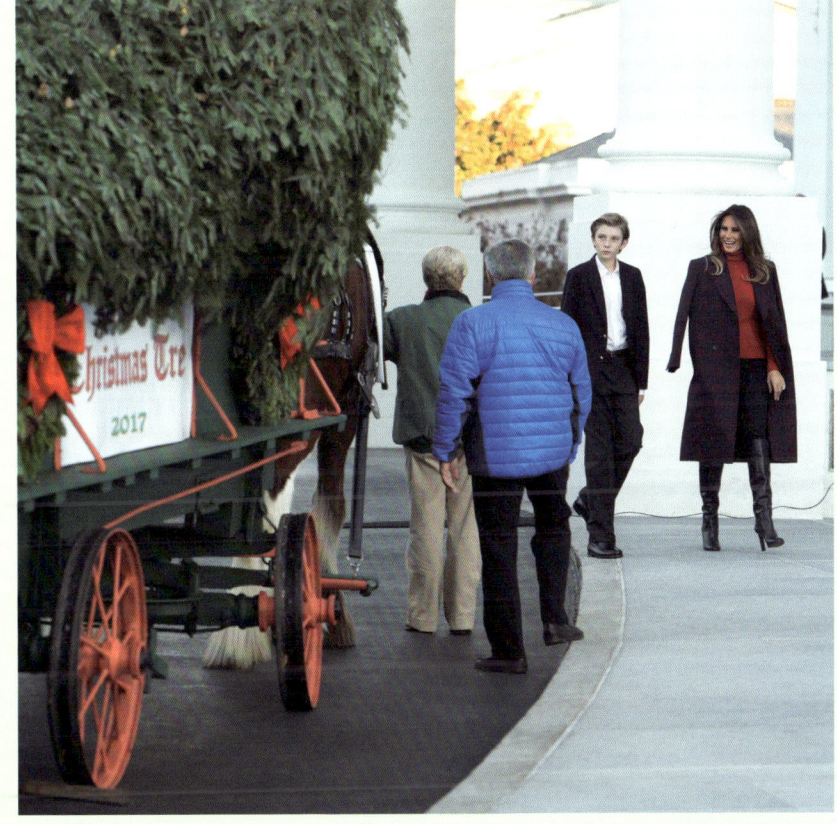

Melania and Barron greet the official White House Christmas Tree, 2017.

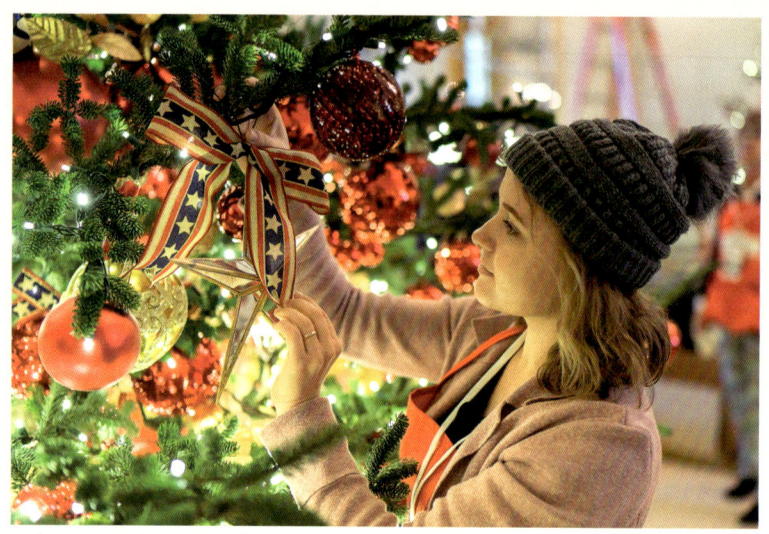

Volunteers decorate the White House for the Christmas season, 2019.

Day. Honoring the folks who sacrifice their time and effort for our country has become an important holiday tradition.

As is tradition, throughout her time in the White House, Melania has been the primary force behind the themed decorations that signal the holiday season—from the display of the official White House tree to the adornments in each and every room. After becoming First Lady of the United States in 2017, Melania Trump took on the Christmastime responsibility of ensuring no corner of the White House was left bare once she was through with it. Each room's theme represents an aspect of the majesty of the United States, its people, or past presidents. One can see clearly the style and elegance she learned from her mother, the influence of the designers she has modeled for, and the family's rich cultural background, alongside the traditions picked up from First Ladies past. These have not only influenced how the Trumps spend Christmas with Barron but also now contribute to celebrations of Christmas with the nation during her White House years.

Christmas is a time of love, stress, worship, and traditions. After Thanksgiving, the decorations come out and music blares from the local shopping center. Baking menus are planned with a variety of cookies, candies, and treats, most of which have been passed down from that one grandmother who was the best cook in the family. Melania's White House reflects a global tradition that is unique in American history, as she is only the second First Lady who was not born in the United States and the first who is a naturalized citizen. Despite their financial standing, the Trumps are just like us when it comes to how they celebrate Christmas. We go to church, we pray, we thank God for His Son, we feast, and we give gifts. These are rich traditions we all have in common no matter where you are from.

"Every American heart is thankful to you, and we're asking God to watch over you and to watch over your families."

Continue on this photographic journey with us as we take a look through the beauty and elegance of Christmases at the White House past, guided by Melania's graceful hand. One can only await with anticipation the theming and beauty of Christmas at the White House during this second term.

Time Honored Traditions

2017

The First Family will celebrate their first Christmas in the White House with a nod to tradition. This year's theme, "Time Honored Traditions," was designed by First Lady Melania Trump to pay respect to 200 years of holiday traditions at the White House.

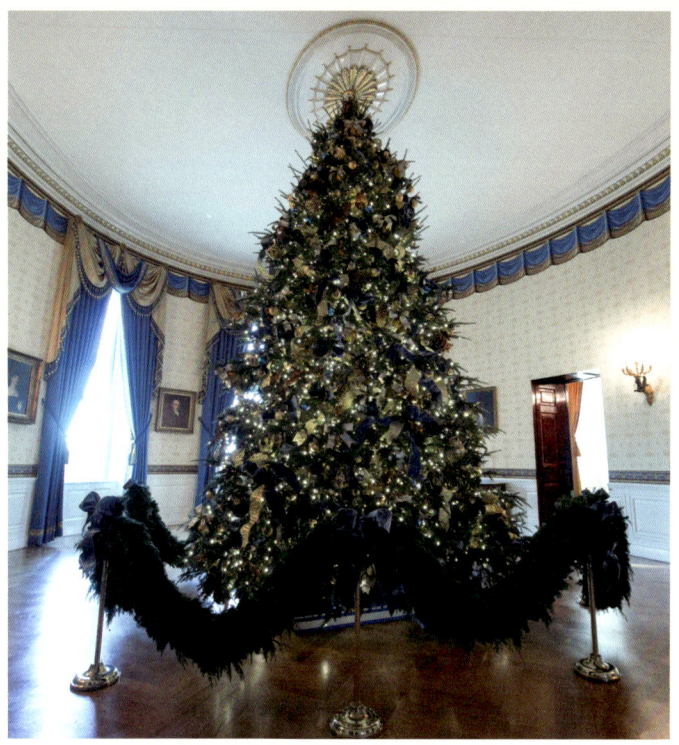

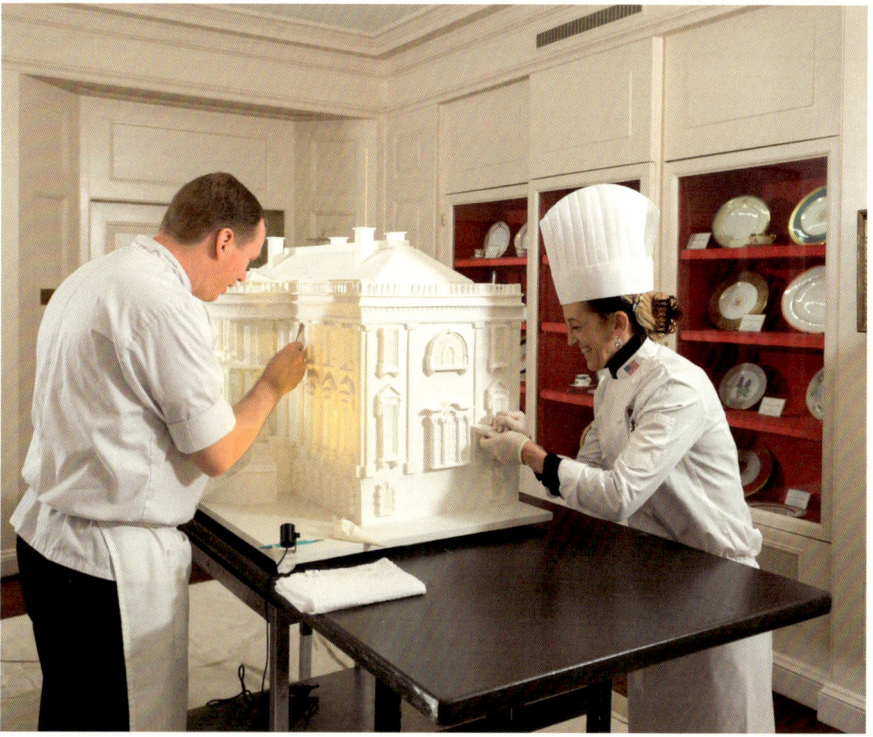

The White House Christmas Tree is seen in the Blue Room during a preview of holiday decorations at the White House. (Photo by Saul Loeb/AFP via Getty Images)

The White House Pastry Team works on the official Gingerbread House for 2017.

In the East Wing, there was a tribute to America's service members and their families. The centerpiece is the Gold Star Family Tree, a tradition since 2011. The tree is decorated with patriotic ribbons and gold wooden stars engraved with the names of fallen service members. Digital tablets are provided, and visitors are encouraged to write a message to their loved ones overseas.

Through the East Colonnade is the China Room, which honored the traditions of dining and hospitality. The room was set up for Christmas dinner using china provided by President Ronald Reagan. The library featured President Franklin D. Roosevelt's 1866 edition of *A Christmas Carol*, hearkening back to memories of reading Christmas stories to children.

On the State Floor, the Grand Foyer and Cross Hall celebrate the first themed Christmas at the White House, the "Nutcracker Suite" in 1961. The Green Room celebrated the festivities with crafts, paper, and classic design. The Blue Room held the official White House Christmas tree, which was decorated with glass ornaments bearing the seals of each state and territory. The Red Room offered an array of holiday treats—peppermints, cookies, and candy. In the State Dining Room, a gingerbread house depicted the South facade of the White House and was accompanied by the First Lady's signature Christmas wreaths.

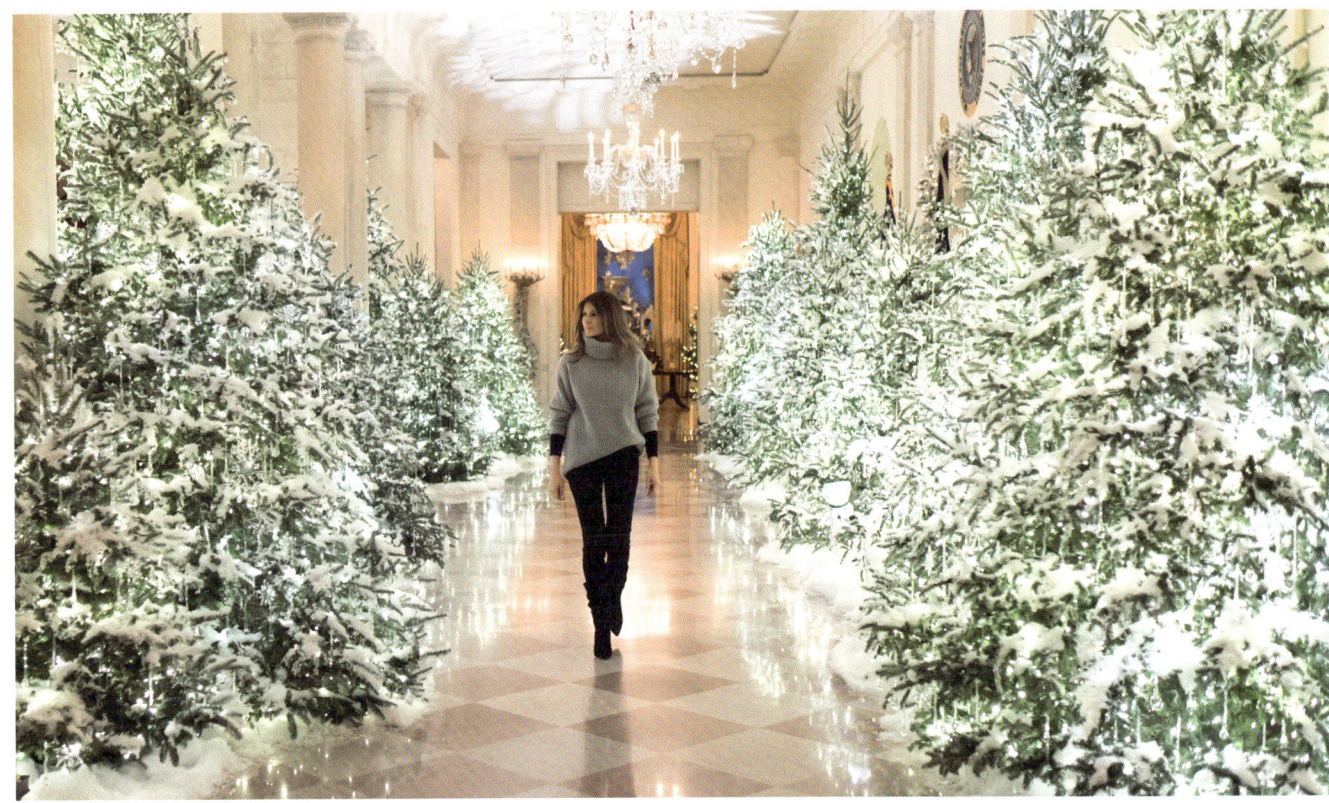

The First Lady takes a last look at the 2017 Christmas decorations of the White House before the previews begin!

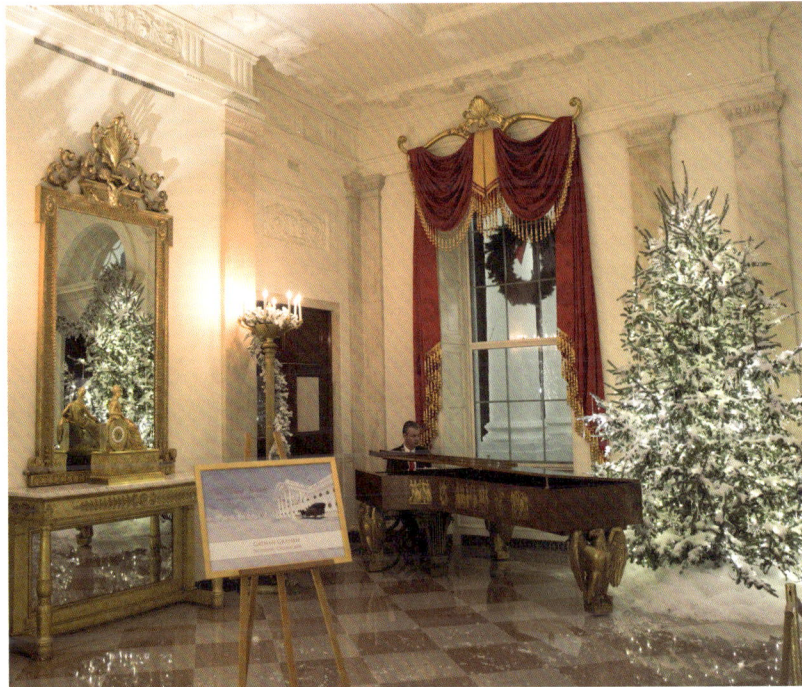

Pianist Gathan Graham performs in the Grand Foyer of the White House. (Official White House Photo by Keegan Barber)

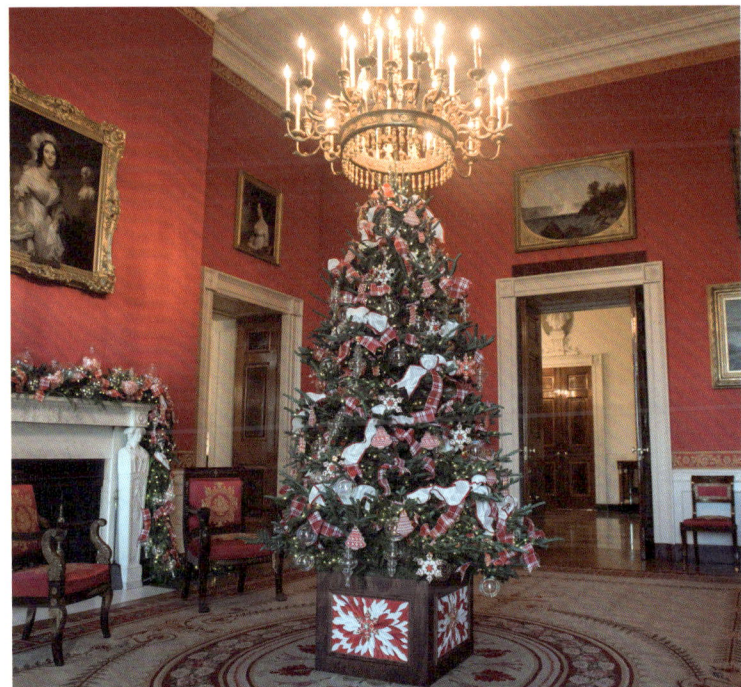

Christmas decorations are seen in the Red Room, which has been decorated with peppermints, candy, and cookies. (Photo by Saul Loeb/AFP via Getty Images)

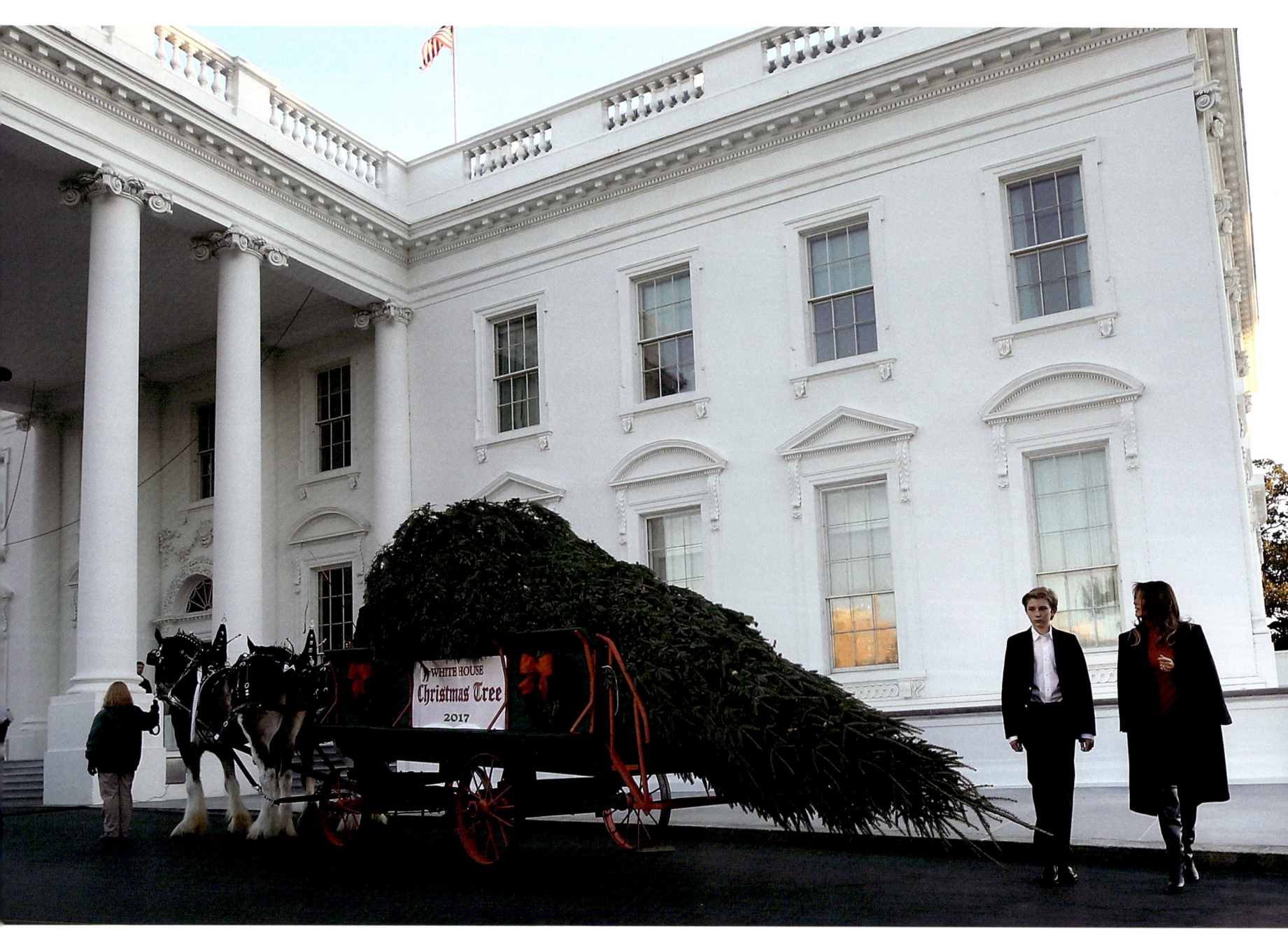

First lady Melania Trump and her son Barron inspect the 19.5-foot Balsam Fir that will serve as the official White House Christmas Tree. The tree is a Wisconsin grown fir provided by the Chapman family of Silent Night Evergreens. (Photo by Mark Wilson/Getty Images)

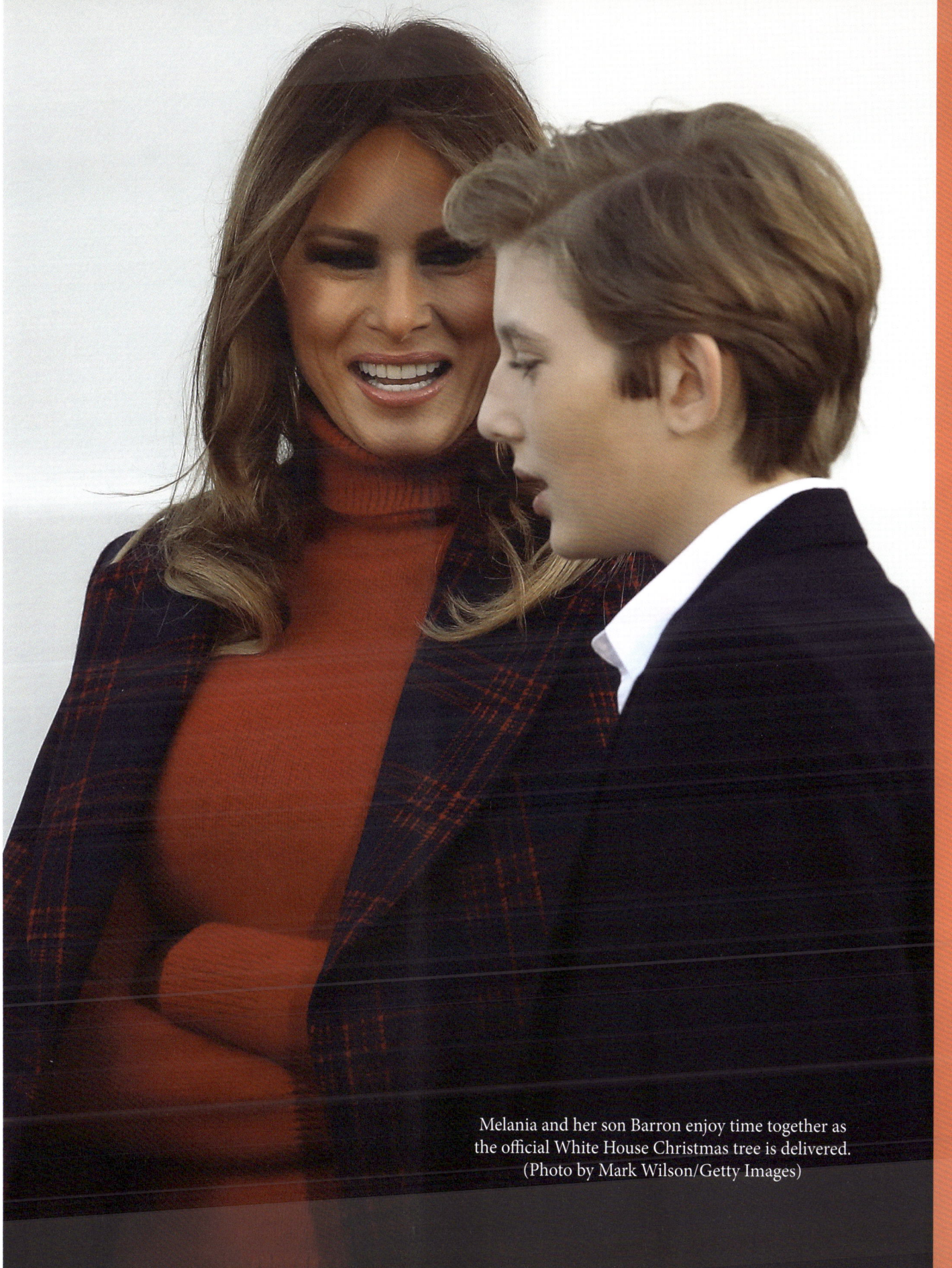

Melania and her son Barron enjoy time together as the official White House Christmas tree is delivered. (Photo by Mark Wilson/Getty Images)

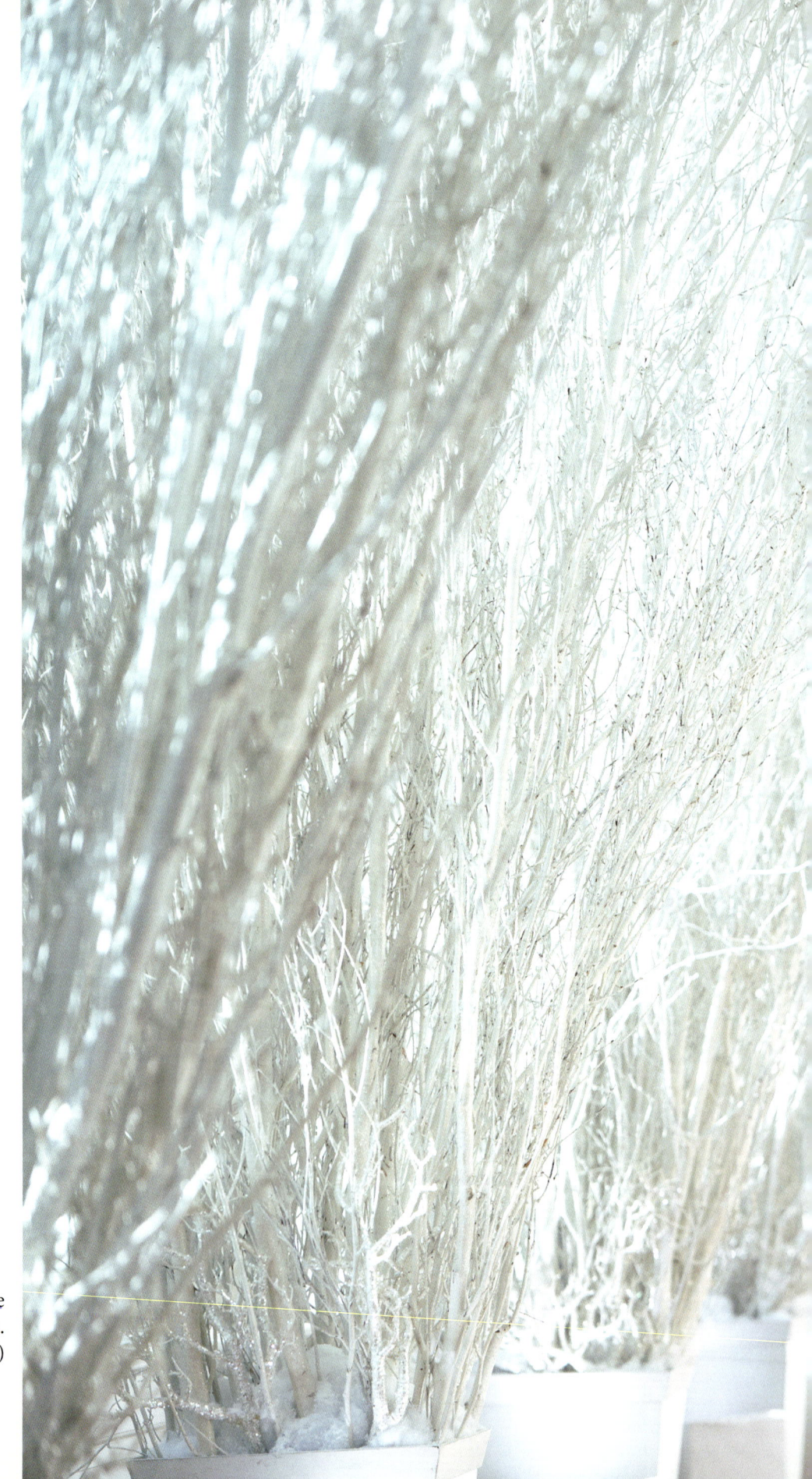

The First Lady's elegance lights up with the trees in the East Wing of the White House. (Photo by Saul Loeb/AFP/Getty Images)

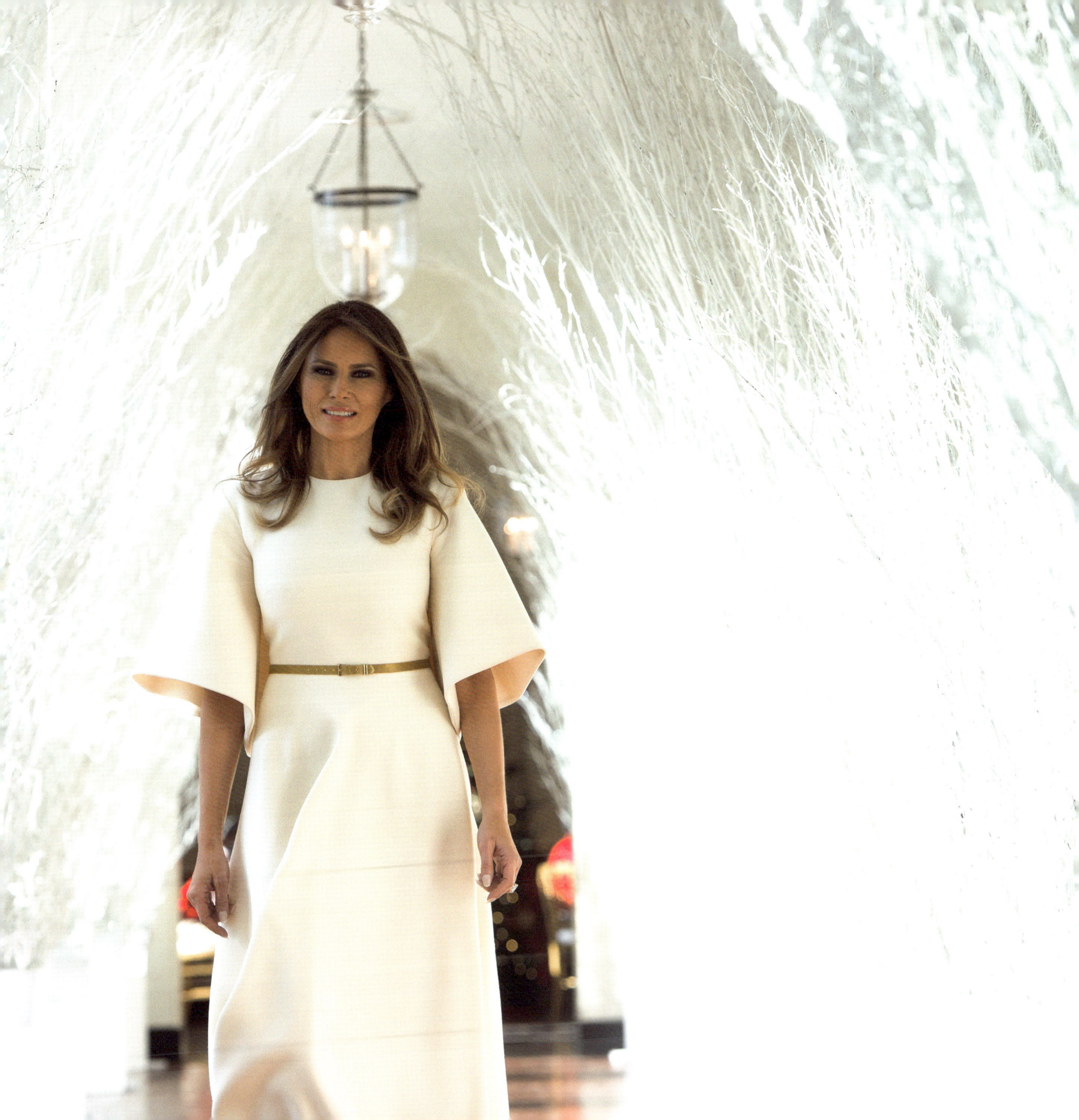

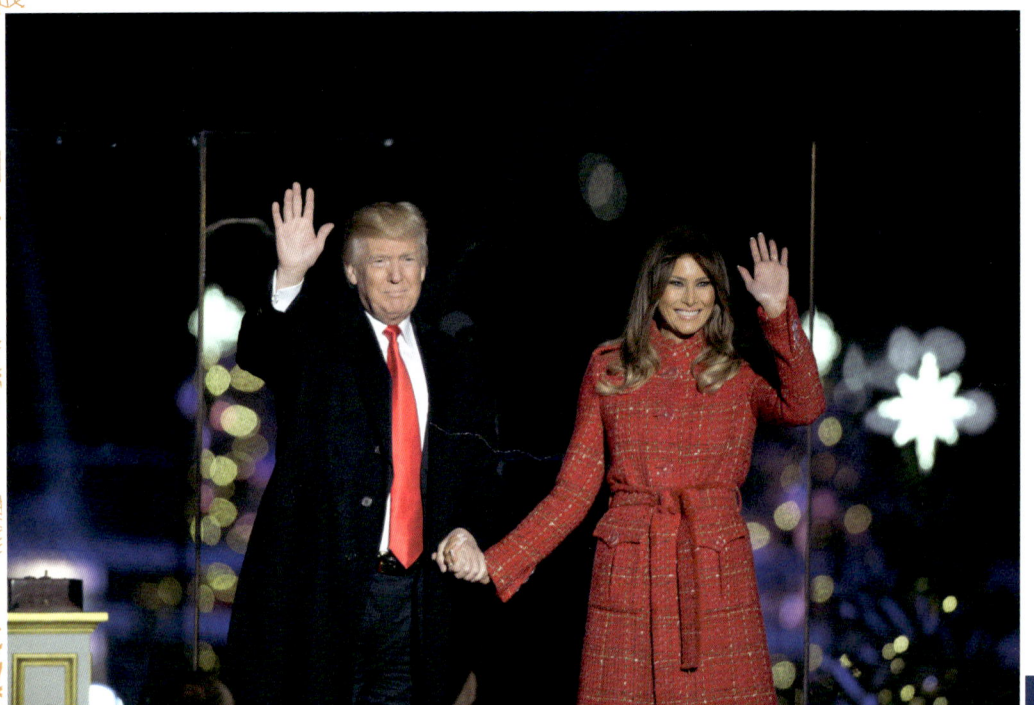

Left: Waving to the crowd at the 95th annual Christmas tree lighting ceremony. (Official White House Photo by Joyce N. Boghosian)

Below: The official tree all lit up for the season! (Official White House Photo by Joyce N. Boghosian)

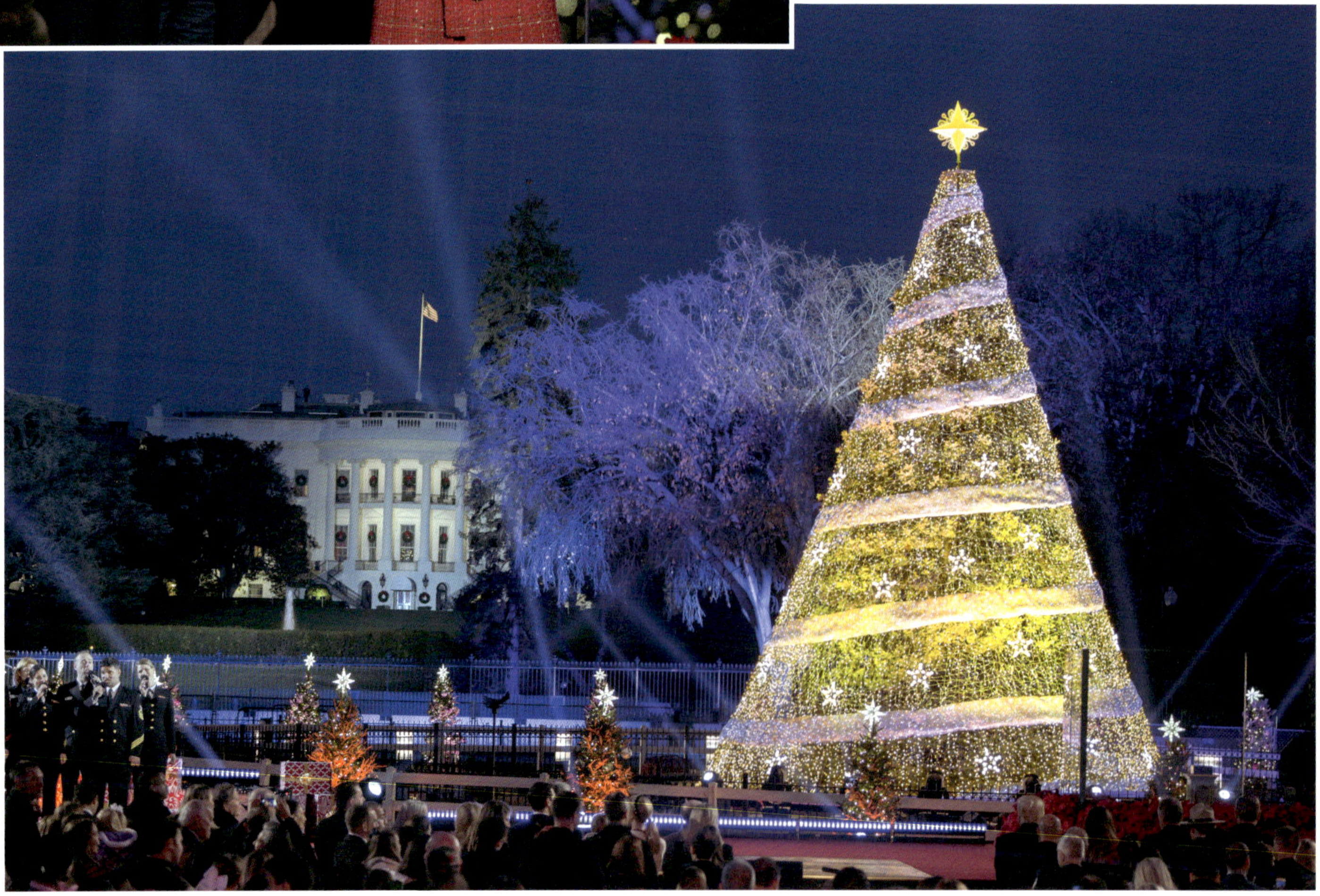

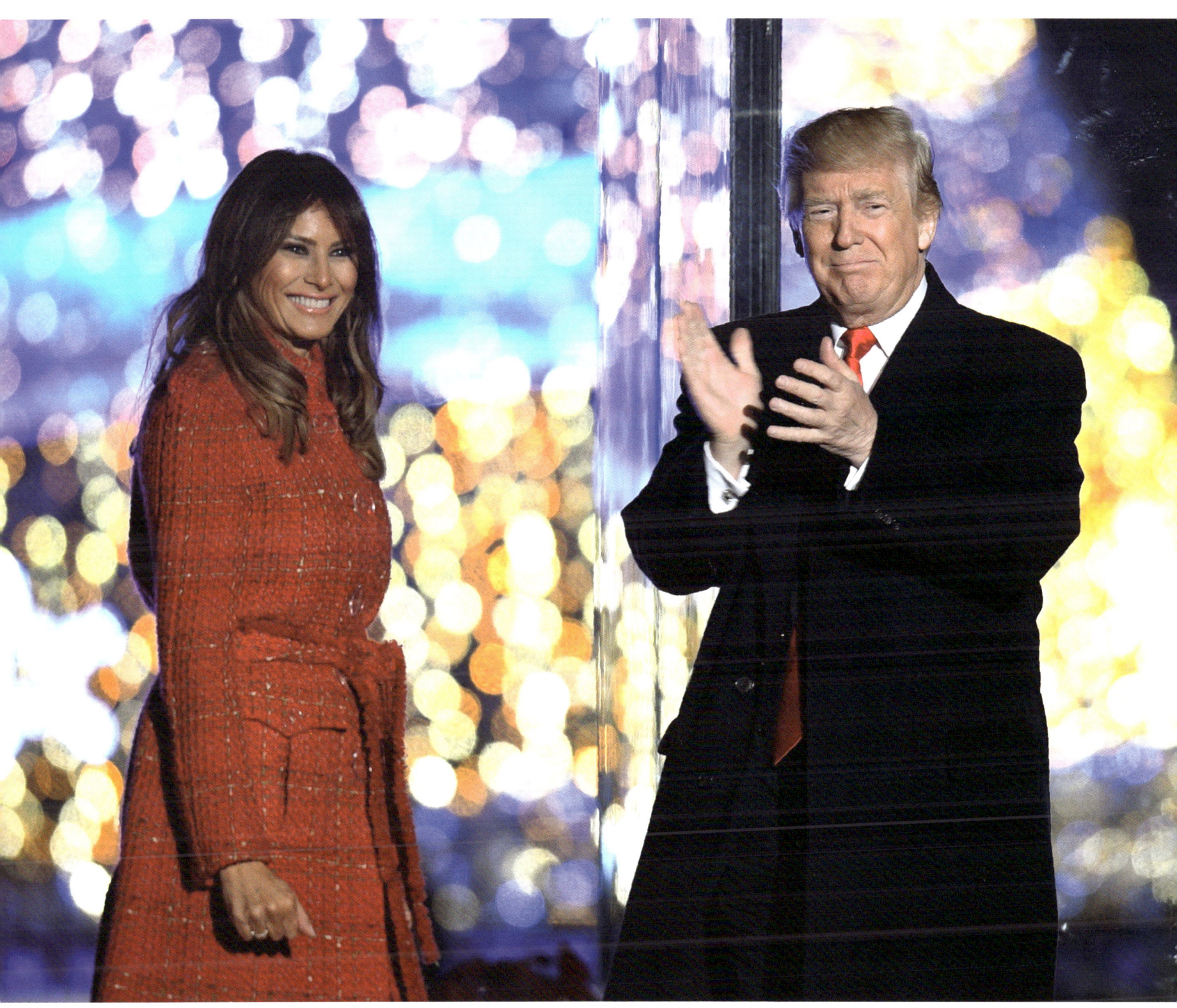

The President and First Lady preside over the annual Christmas tree lighting ceremony. (Photo by Jim Watson/AFP/Getty Images)

"The President, Barron, and I are very excited for our first Christmas in the White House. As with many families across the country, holiday traditions are very important to us. I hope when visiting the People's House this year, visitors will get a sense of being home for the holidays. On behalf of my husband and Barron, I want to wish everyone a Merry Christmas and a joyous holiday season."

—First Lady Melania Trump, 2017

President Donald J. Trump and First Lady Melania Trump are seen Tuesday, December 5, in their official 2017 Christmas portrait.

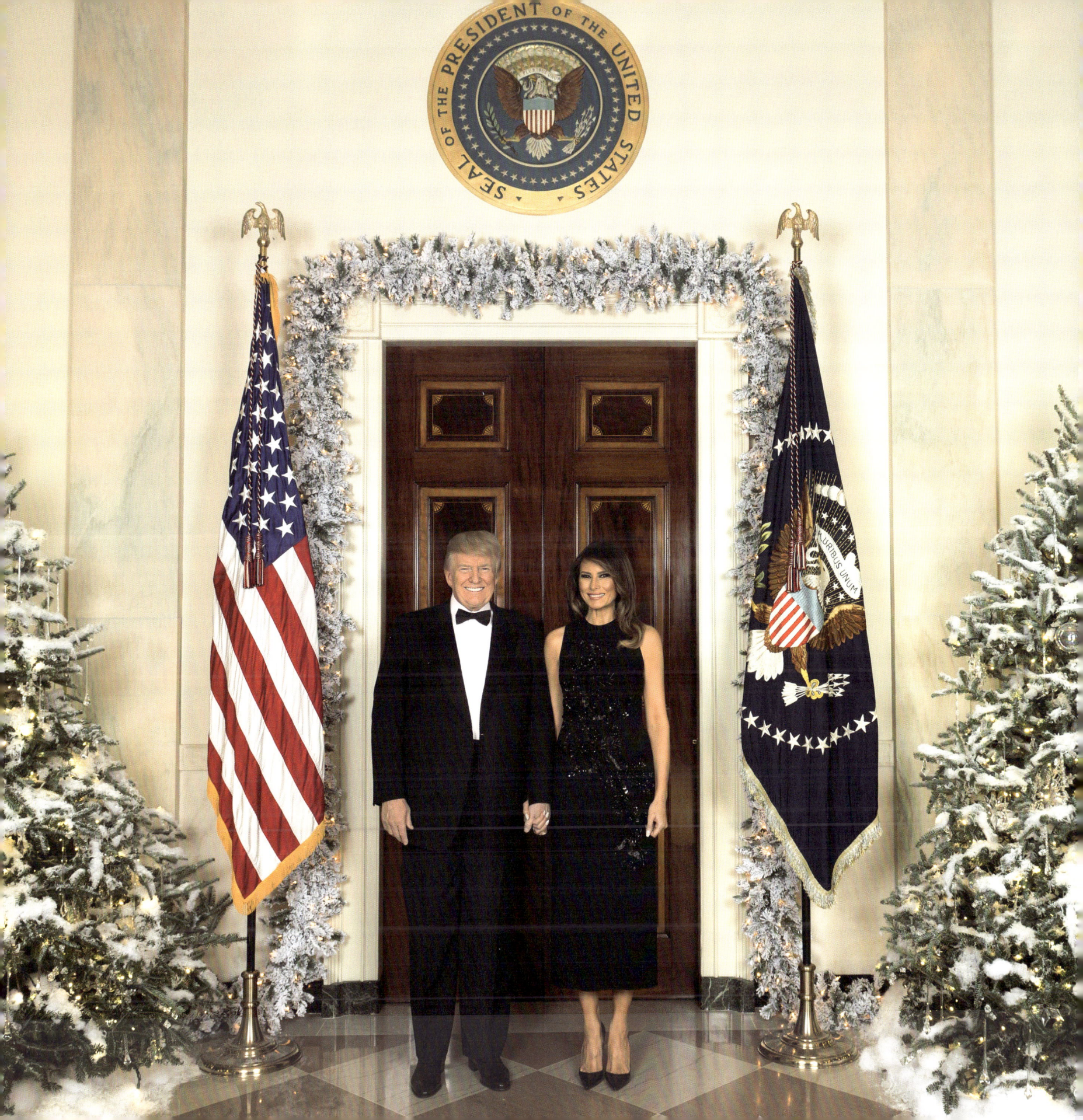

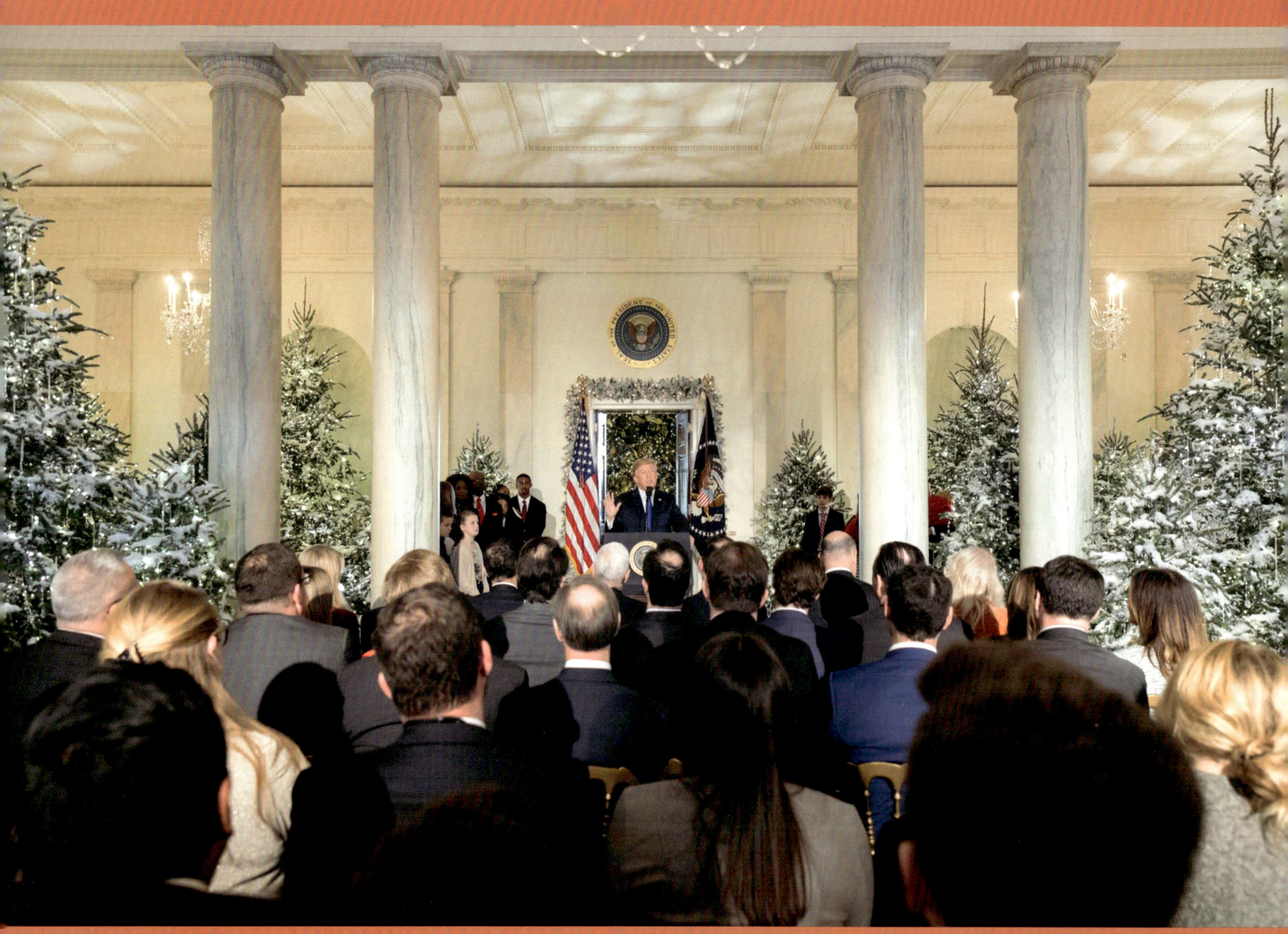

When Christmas comes around, even remarks on the budget and tax cuts happen with a backdrop of holiday cheer!
(Official White House Photo by Stephanie Chasez)

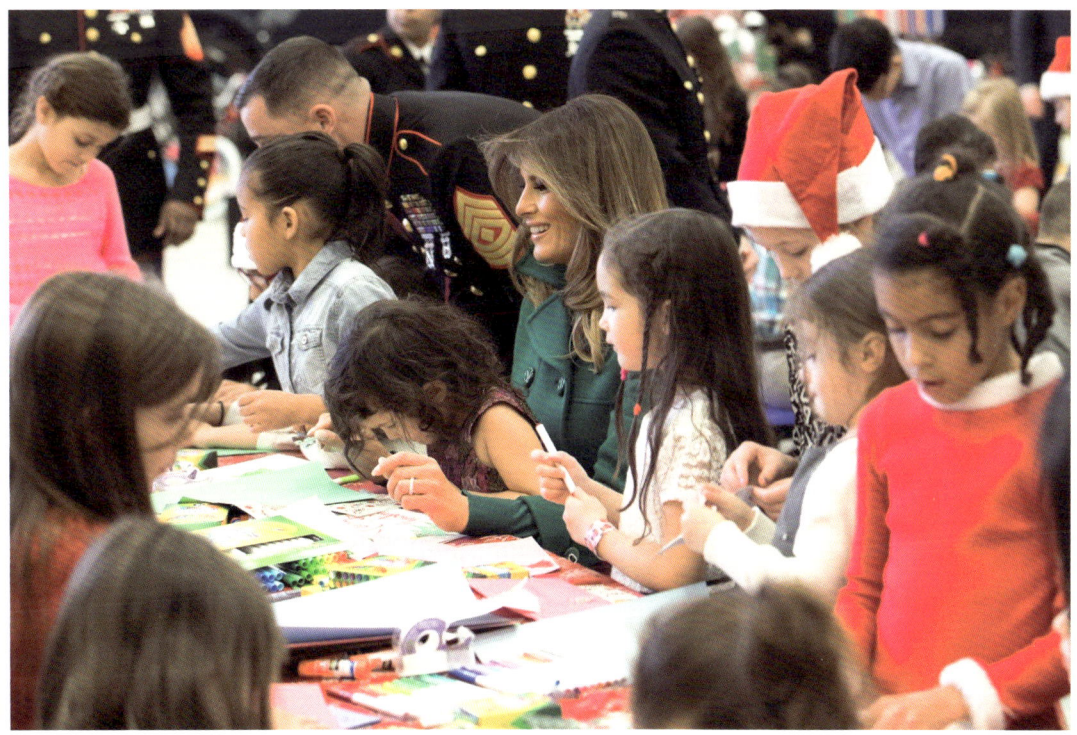

First Lady Melania Trump attends a Toys for Tots event, making cards with the kids at Joint Base Anacostia-Bolling in Washington, D.C.

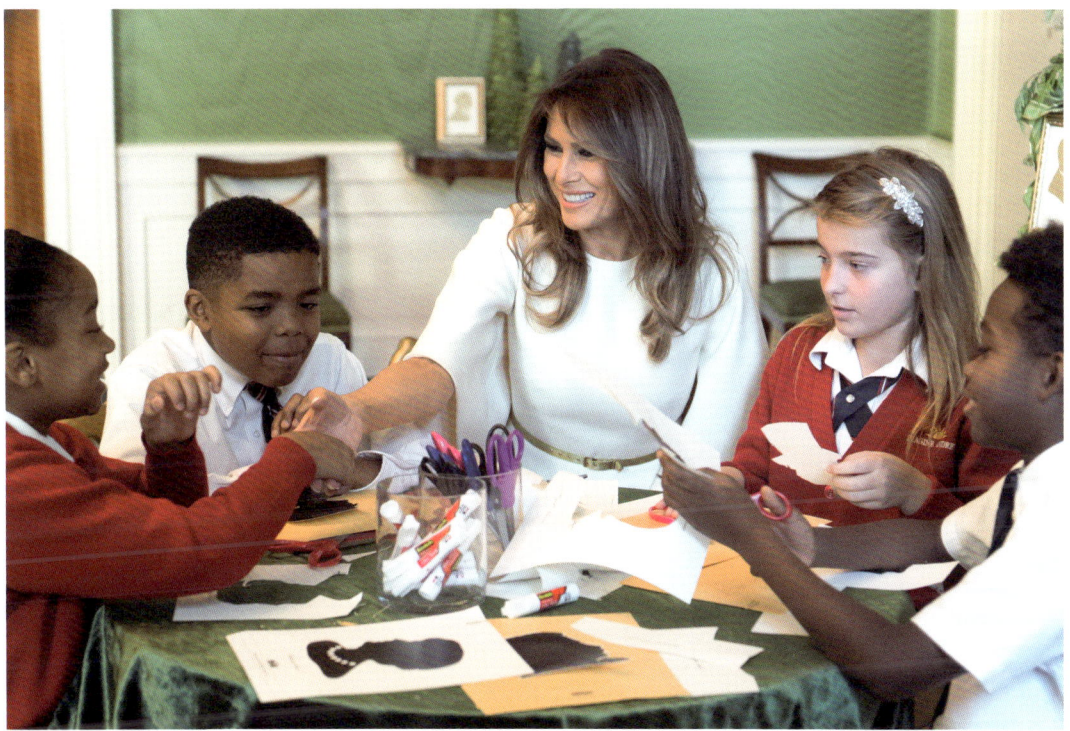

Melania Trump participates in an arts and crafts project with children from Joint Base Andrews, Maryland, during their visit to the White House Christmas preview event.

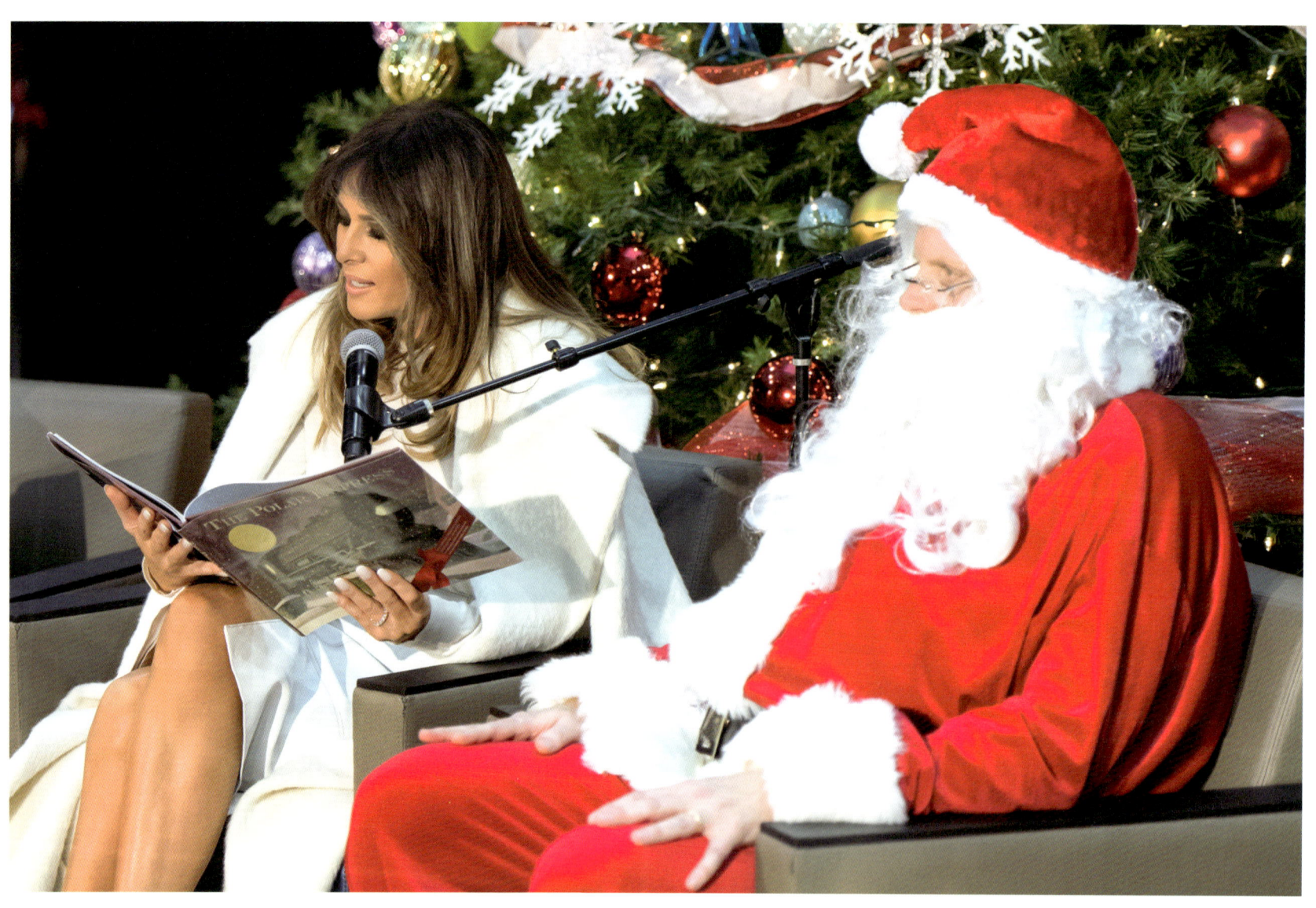

Mrs. Trump reads *The Polar Express* with Santa Claus for the Christmas celebration at Children's National Hospital.

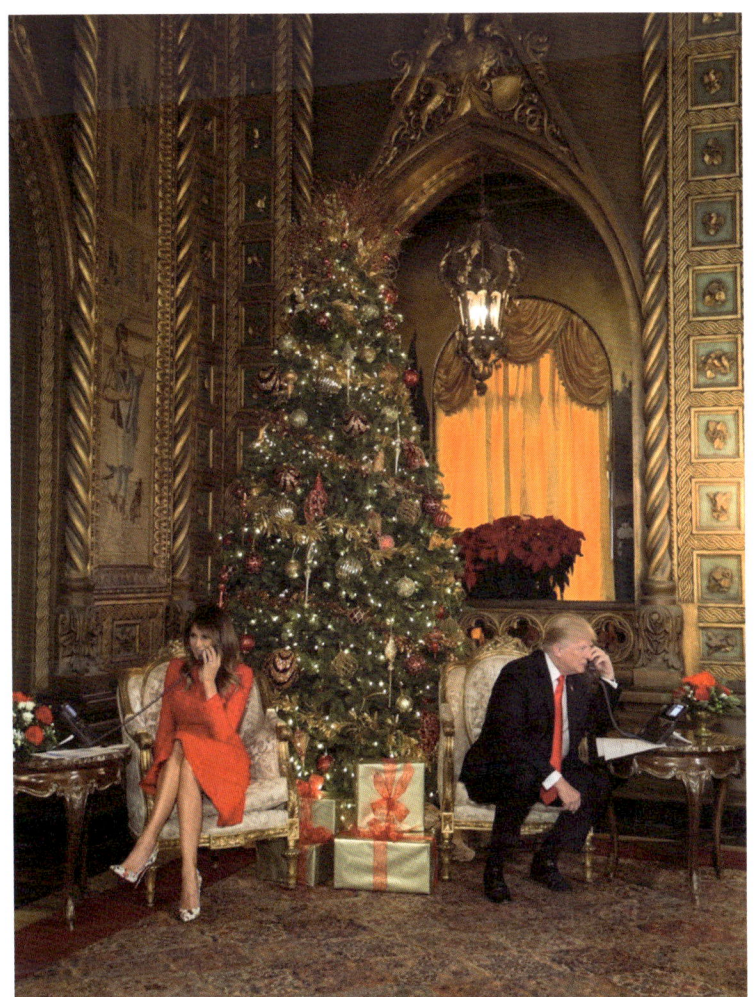

President Trump and the First Lady take phone calls from children in the library of Mar-a-Lago in Palm Beach, Florida, as part of the NORAD Santa Tracker tradition on Christmas Eve, keeping watch on Santa's travels around the world. The First Family asked the children about their Christmas wishes and wished them all a Merry Christmas. (Official White House Photo by Shealah Craighead)

President Donald J. Trump holds a video conference with members of the U.S. military on Christmas Eve, bringing holiday cheer to those who can't be home with their families for the holiday. (Official White House Photo by Shealah Craighead)

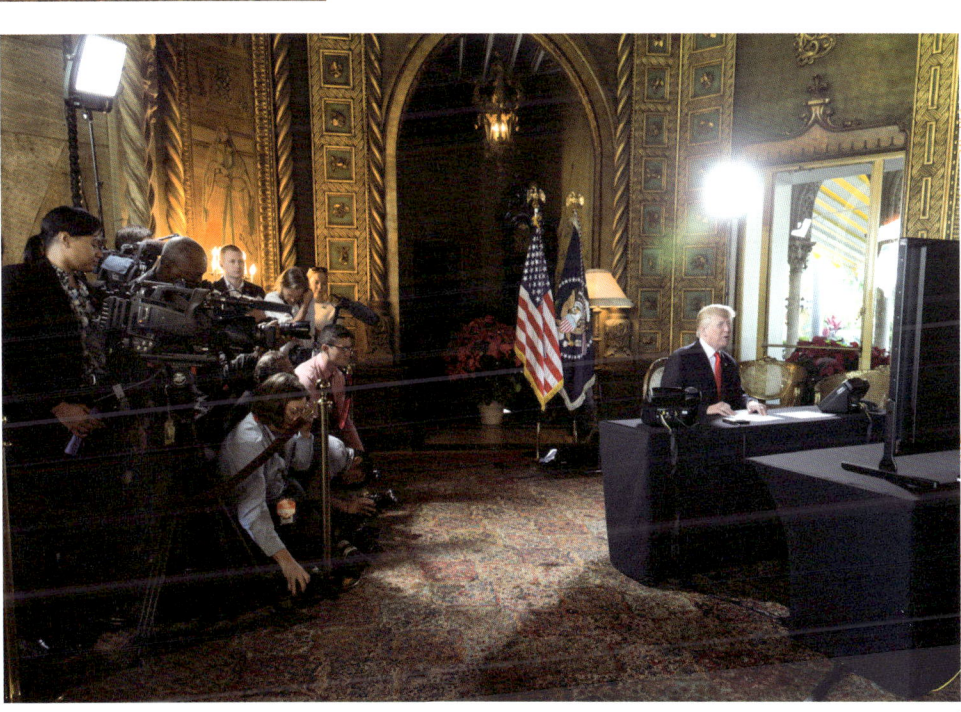

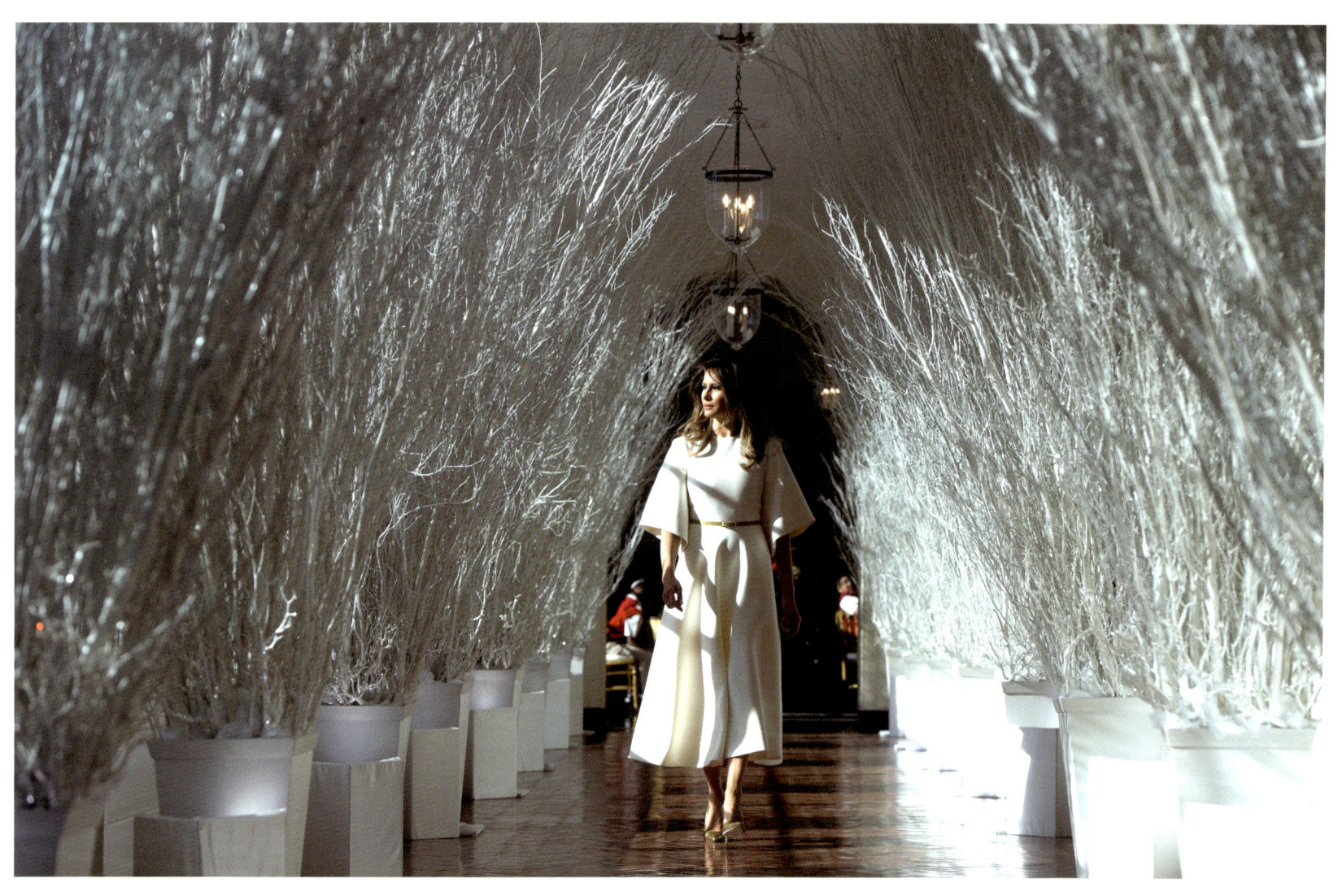

Melania inspects the Christmas decorations in the East Colonnade. (Photo by Saul Loeb/AFP/Getty Images)

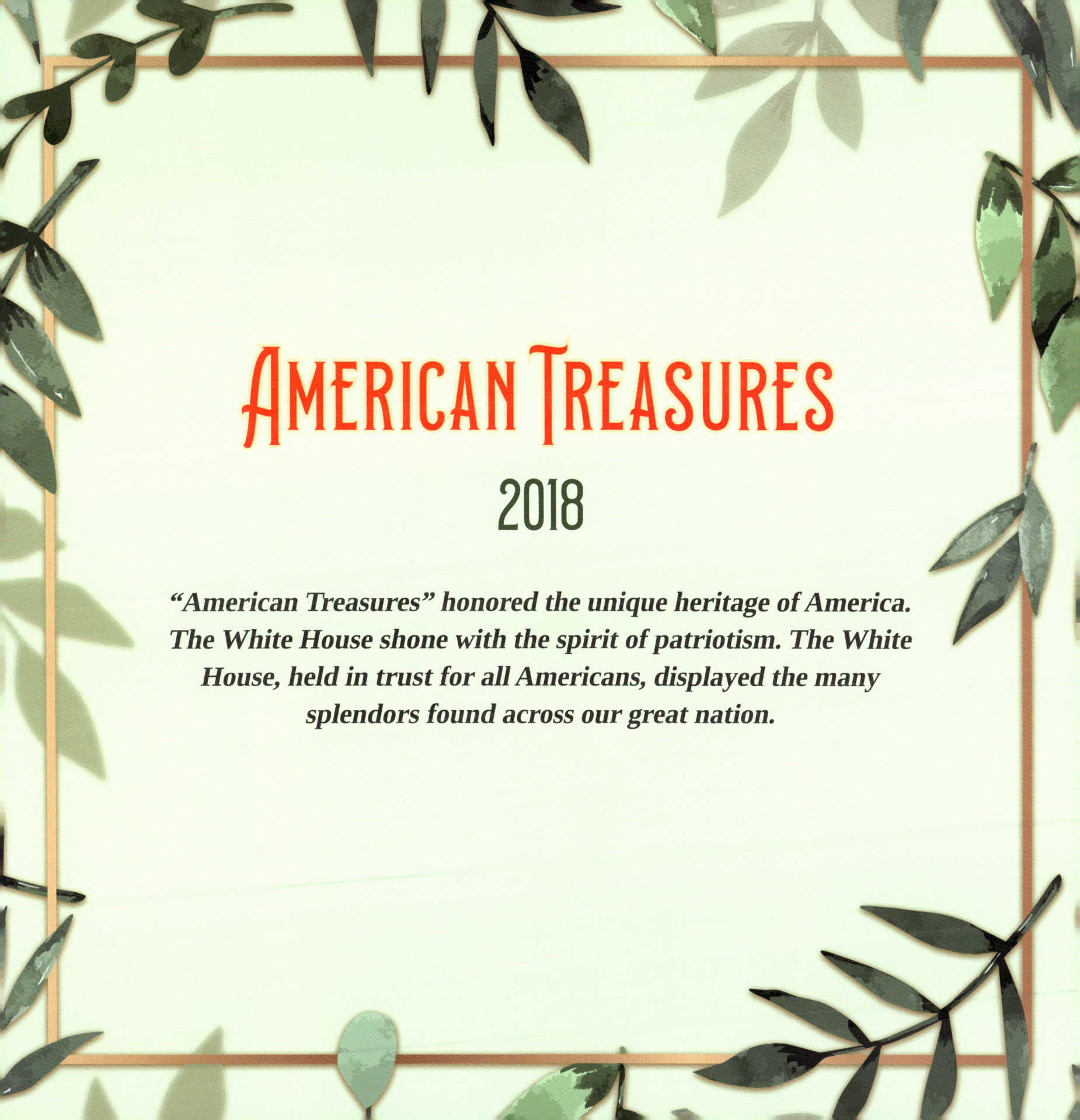

American Treasures

2018

"American Treasures" honored the unique heritage of America. The White House shone with the spirit of patriotism. The White House, held in trust for all Americans, displayed the many splendors found across our great nation.

In the East Wing, the Gold Star Tree returned. Decorated by Gold Star Families, the tree shone with gold stars and vibrant ribbons. The walkway to the East Garden Room, lined with over forty red topiary trees, led the way to the East Room, where the Trump family Christmas card and ornaments were on display. The library had four trees placed in each corner, with a display of the White House Historical Association's 2018 ornament in honor of Harry S. Truman.

In the China Room, three dining tables held replicas of three state dinners on White House permanent china collections, in honor of the Theodore Roosevelt, John F. Kennedy, and Donald J. Trump administrations. The East Room showcased the diversity and inventiveness of American architecture, with four custom mantle pieces reproducing the skylines of New York City, St. Louis, Chicago, and San Francisco. Seventy-two handmade paper ornaments representing six regions across America hung from four fourteen-foot noble fir trees. Throughout the rest of the house, American tradition was displayed with national symbols: bald eagles, the rose, and the oak tree. The 2018 gingerbread house replicated the National Mall.

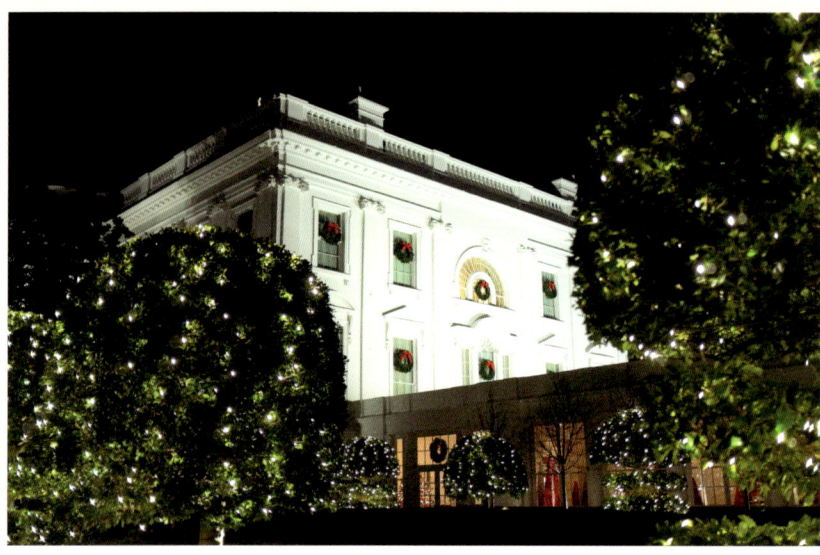

The White House at night with Christmas lighting. (Official White House Photo by Keegan Barber)

In the Grand Foyer and Cross Hall, the theme was patriotism, the heart of America, with more than fourteen thousand red ornaments hanging from four fourteen-foot noble fir trees.

In the Blue Room, the eighteen-foot-tall White House Christmas tree was decorated with five hundred feet of blue velvet ribbon, embroidered in gold with each state and territory. Lastly, in the Red Room, the decor celebrated the children of America and how every one can excel on their own paths toward the future.

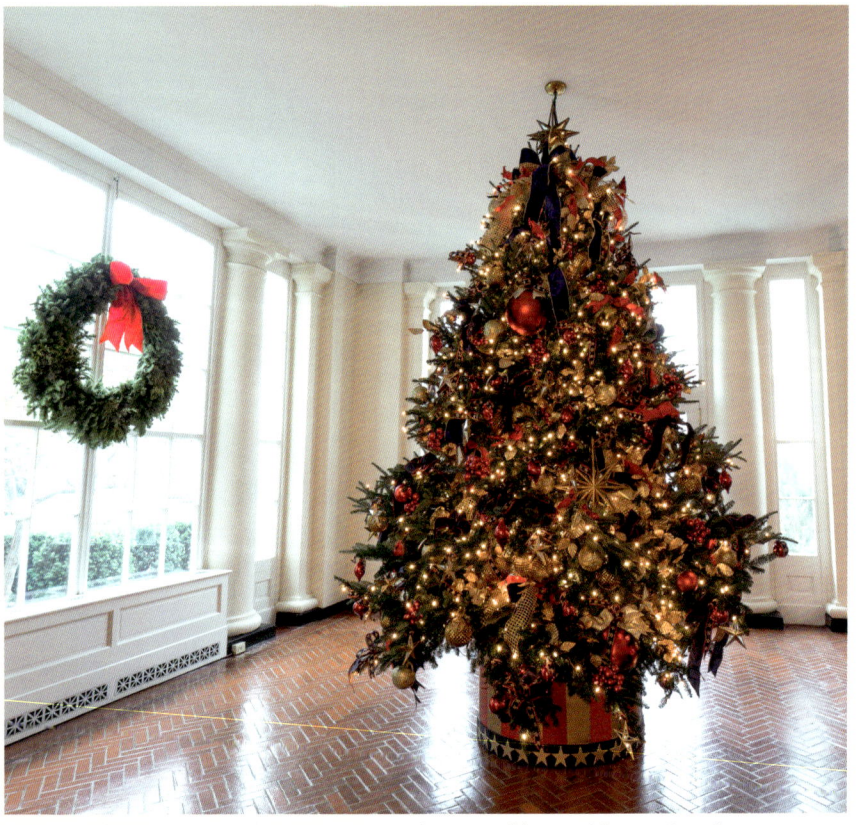

The Gold Star Tree in the East Wing, decorated by Gold Star families.

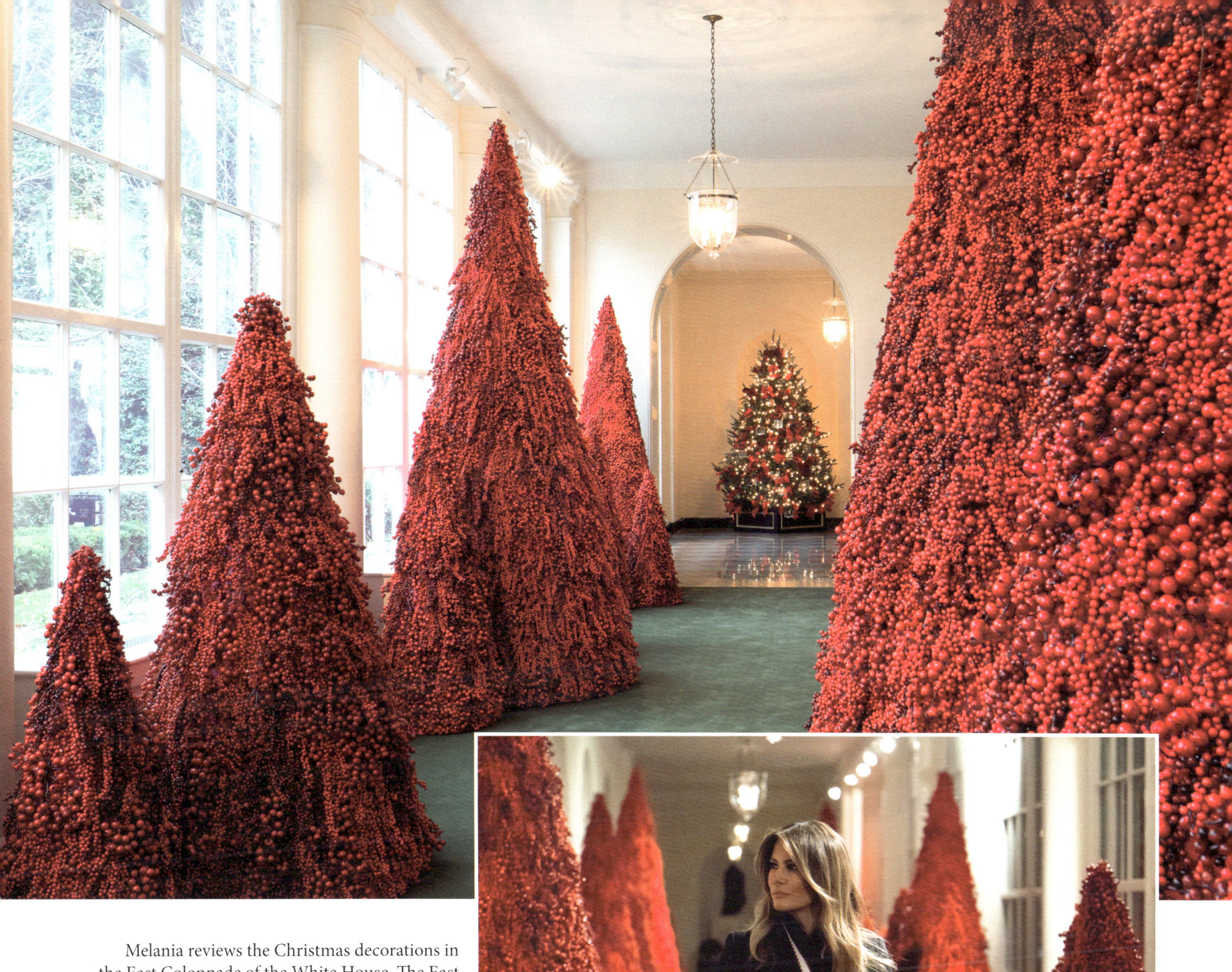

Melania reviews the Christmas decorations in the East Colonnade of the White House. The East Colonnade is decorated with more than forty topiary trees covered in bright red cranberries.

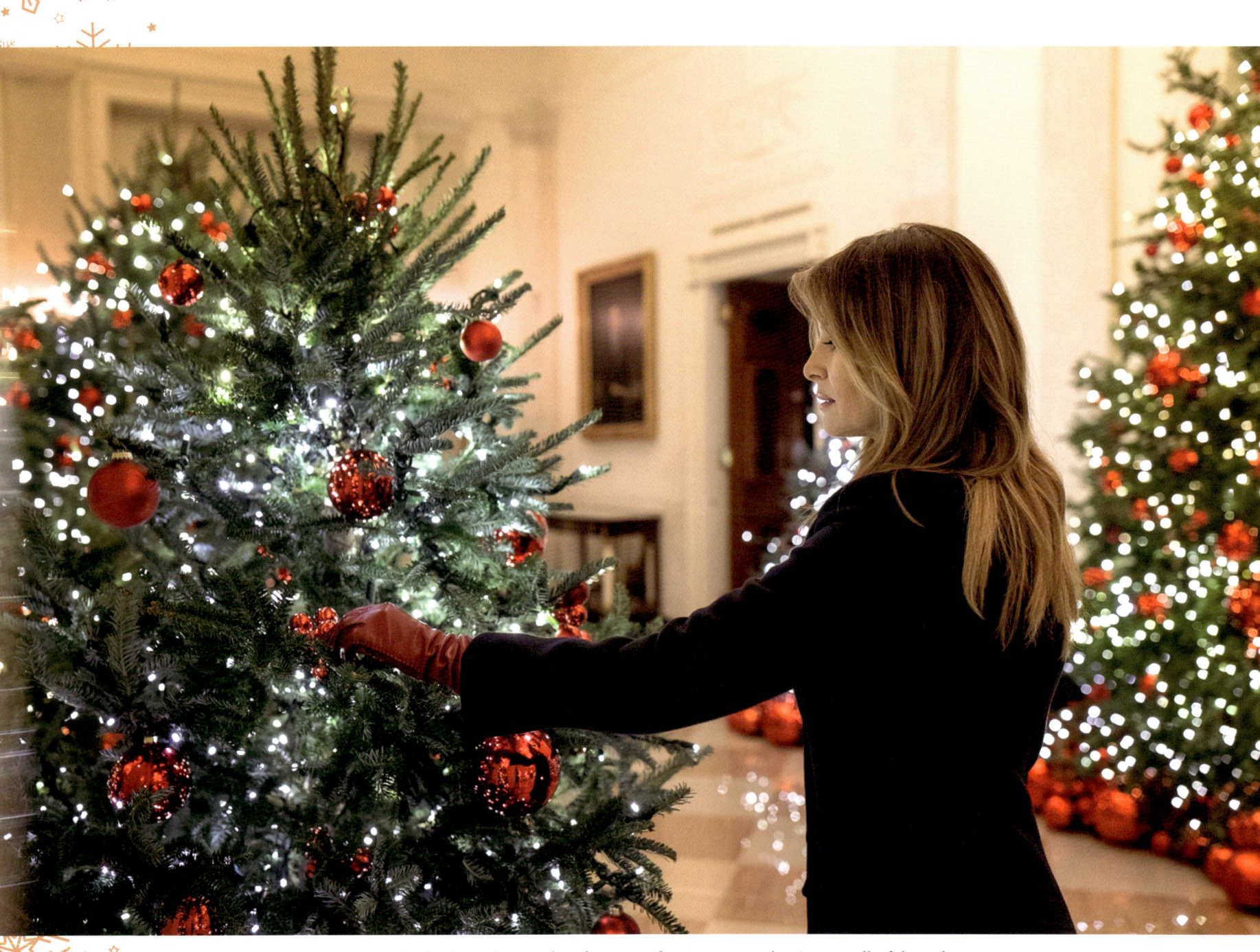

The First Lady does the final touches on the Christmas decorations in the Cross Hall of the White House, which features 14,000 red ornaments across twenty-nine trees.

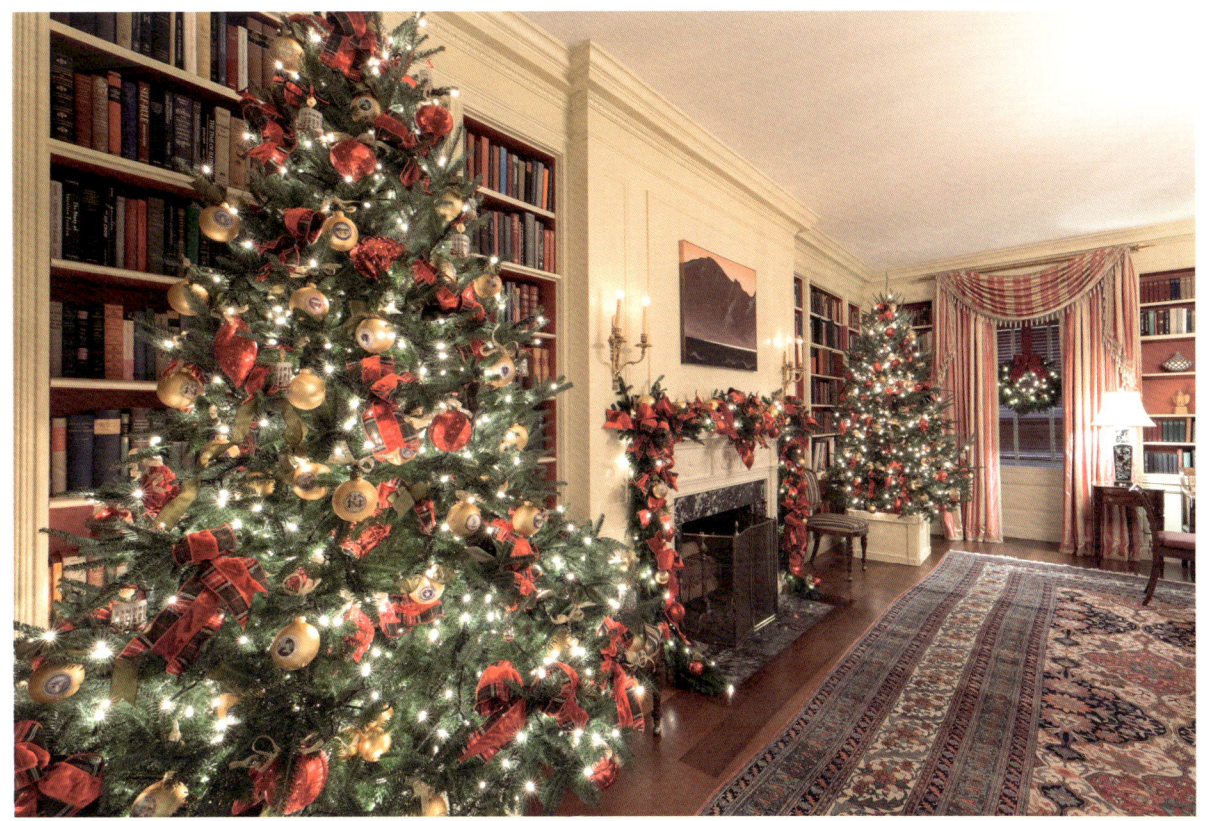

The Library of the White House is decorated for the holiday season, the trees adorned with the White House Historical Association's ornament for 2018.

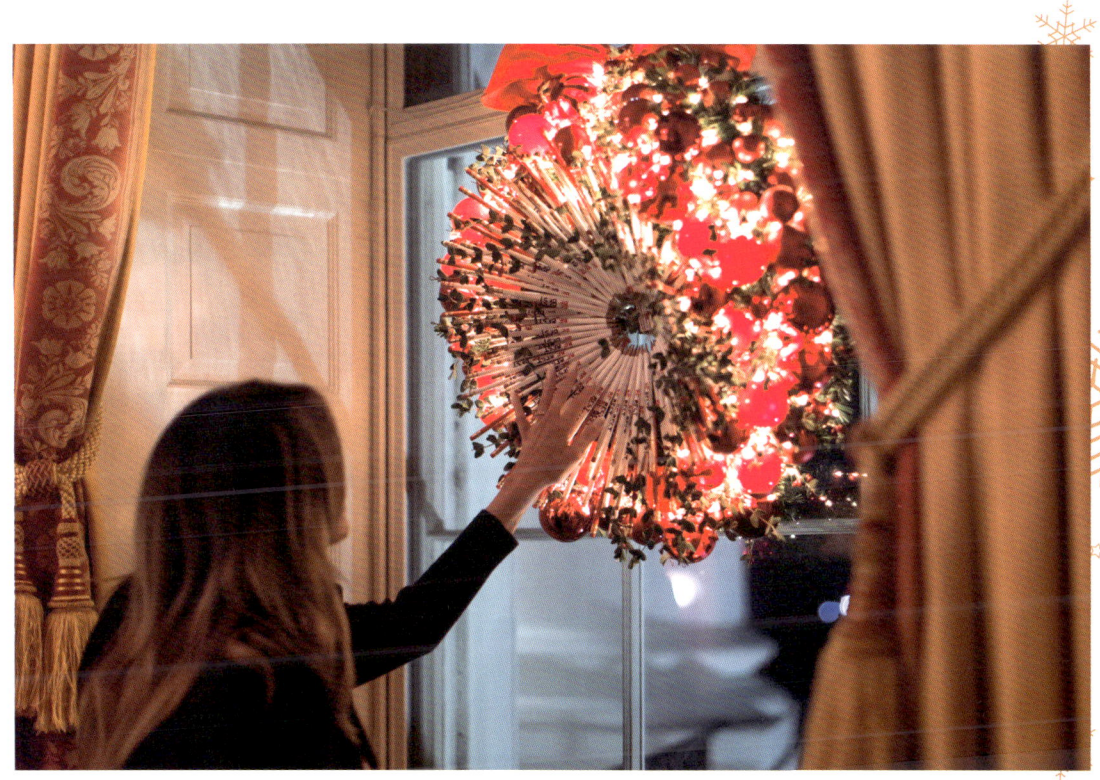

The First Lady's BE BEST campaign extends to her holiday decorations as well! Here she inspects a BE BEST wreath in the Red Room of the White House.

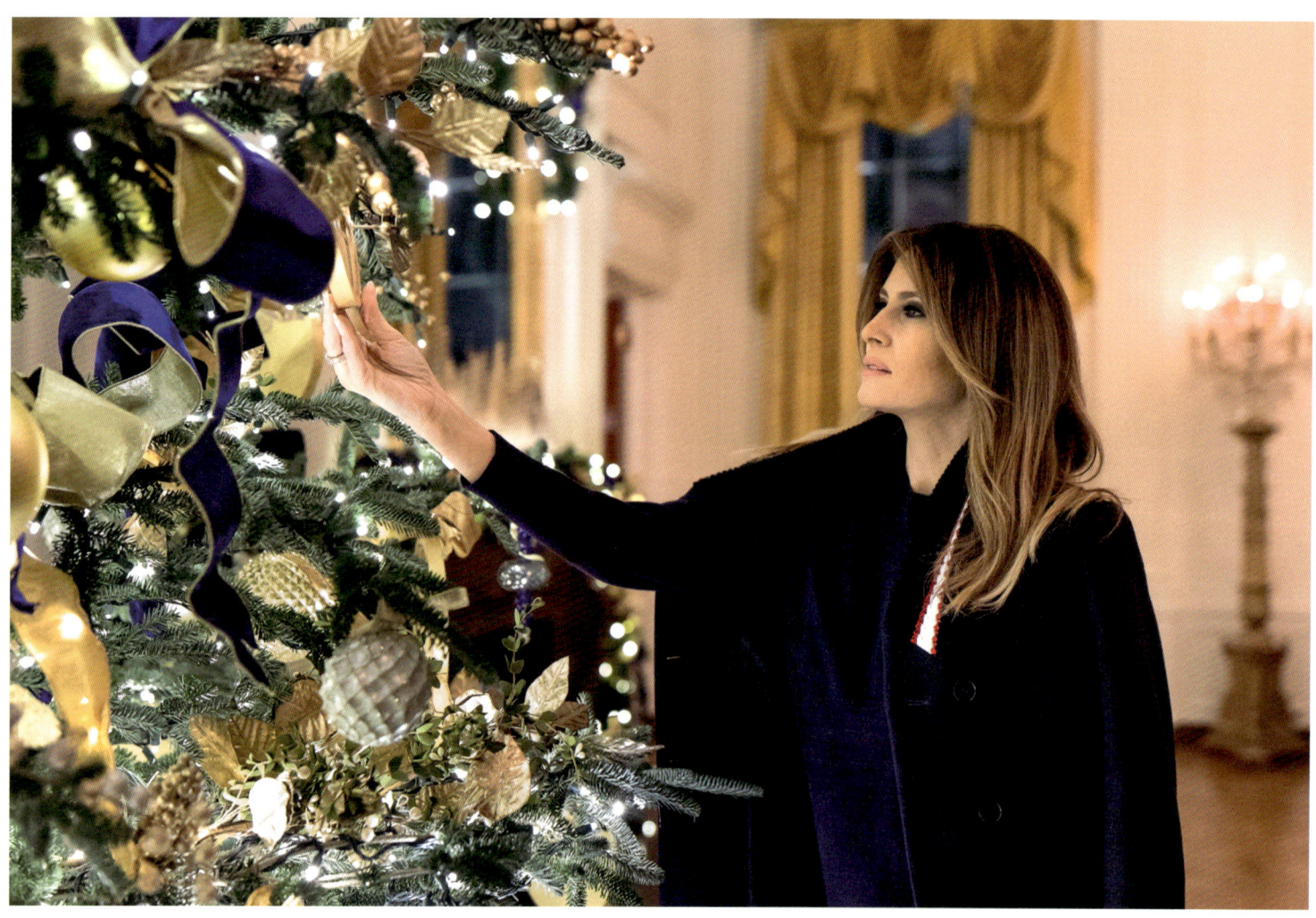

The First Lady reviews decorations in East Room of the White House, which was dedicated this season to the many travelers coming to visit and the ingenuity of American architecture and design. Regionally themed ornaments were hidden among the trees and the mantelpieces each highlighted a different city's iconic architecture.

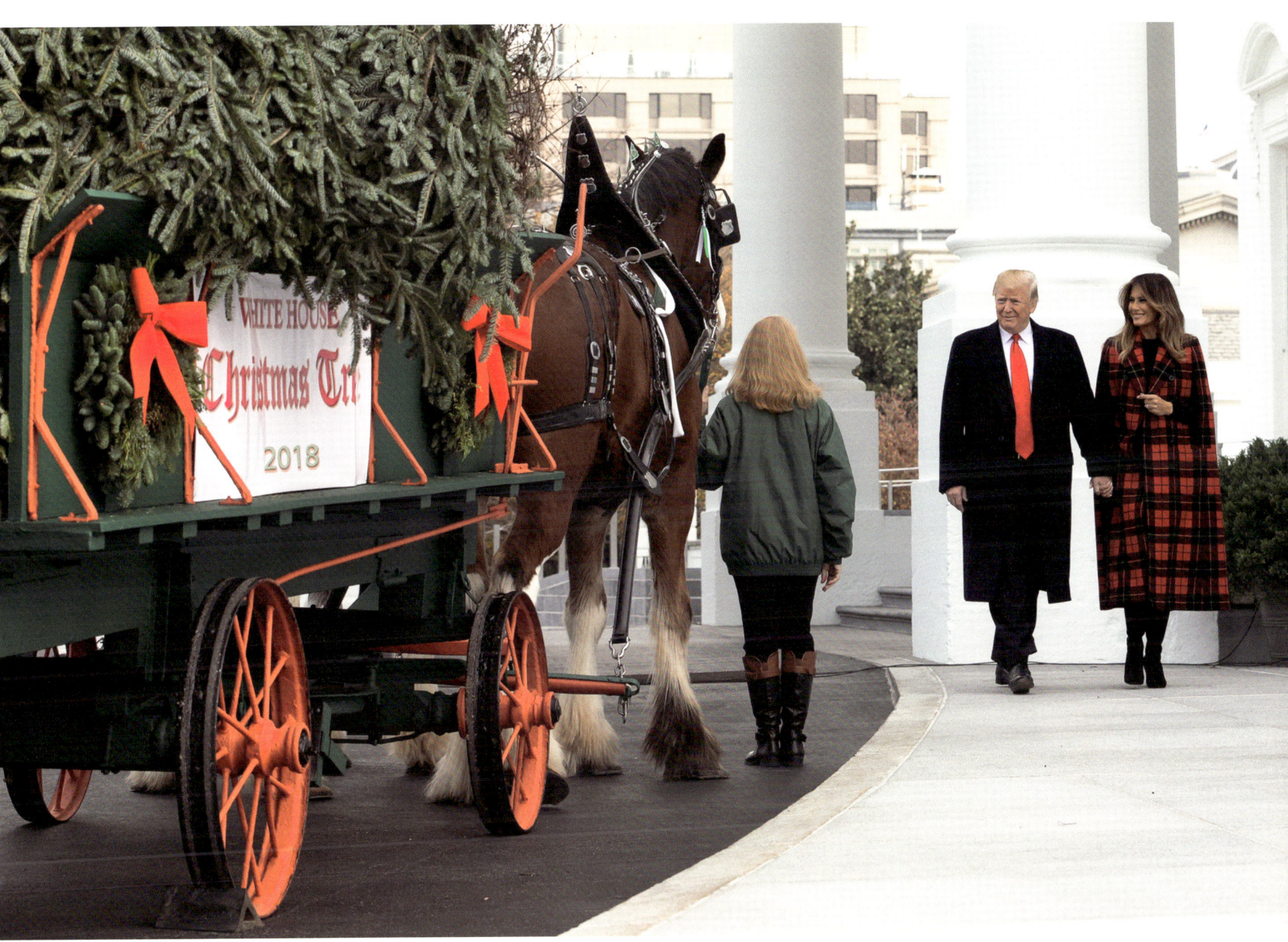

President Donald J. Trump and First Lady Melania Trump receive the White House Christmas Tree at the North Portico of the White House. The tree this year is an 18-foot Fraser Fir from Newland, North Carolina.

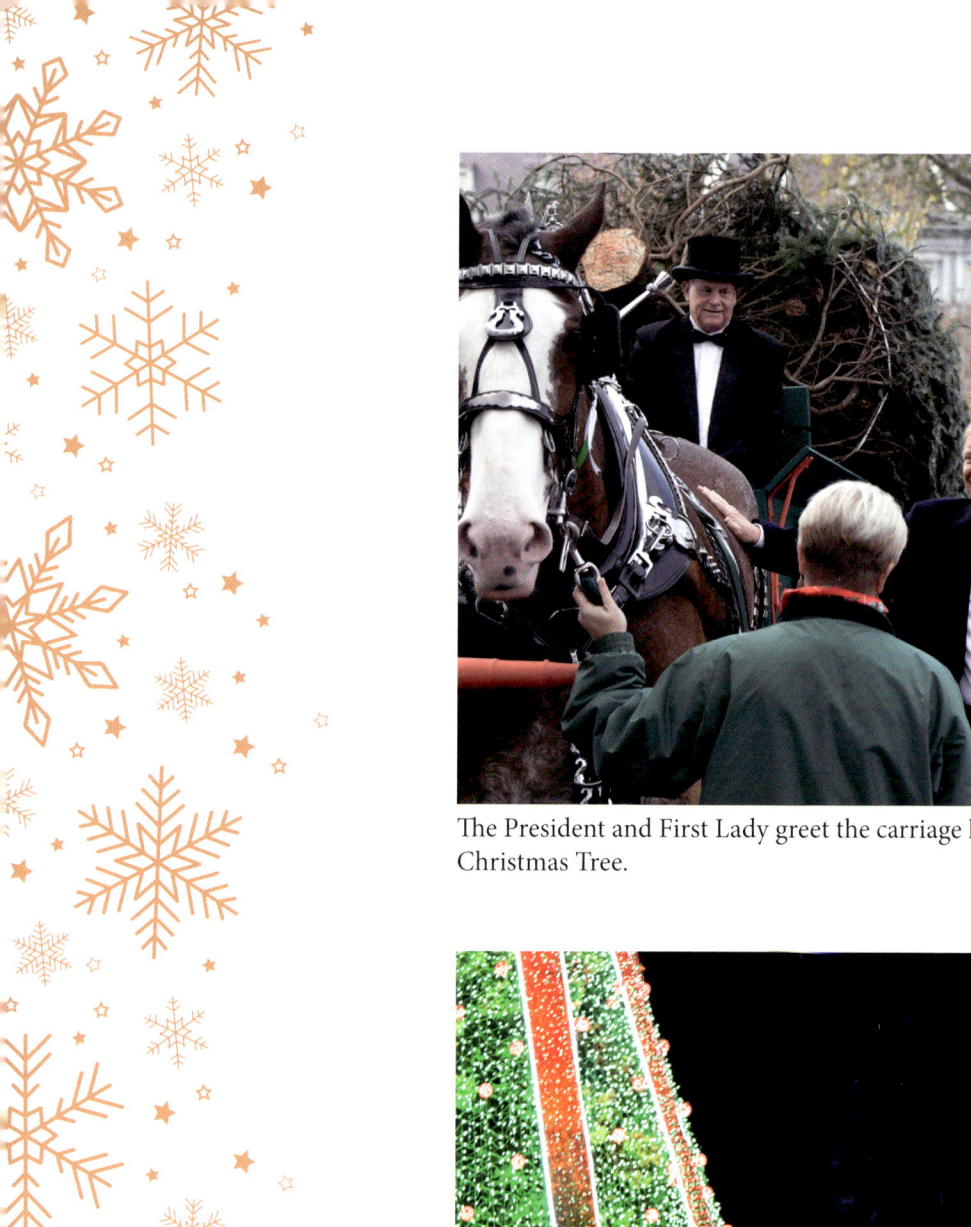

The President and First Lady greet the carriage horses that delivered the White House Christmas Tree.

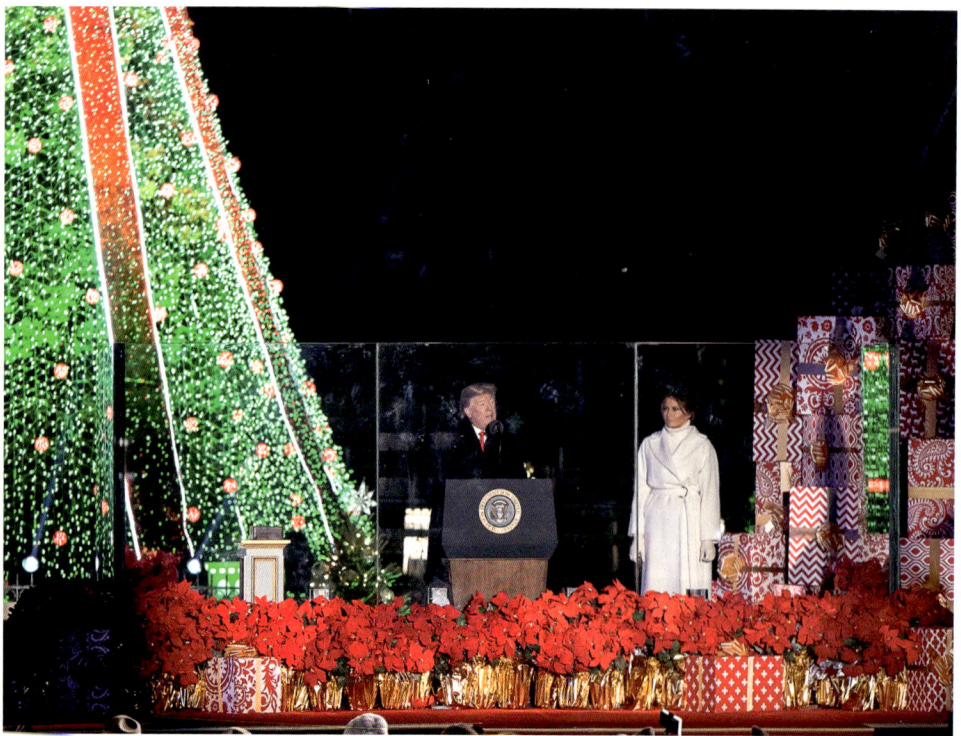

President Donald J. Trump, joined by First Lady Melania Trump, delivers remarks at the National Christmas Tree Lighting Ceremony on the Ellipse in Washington, D.C.

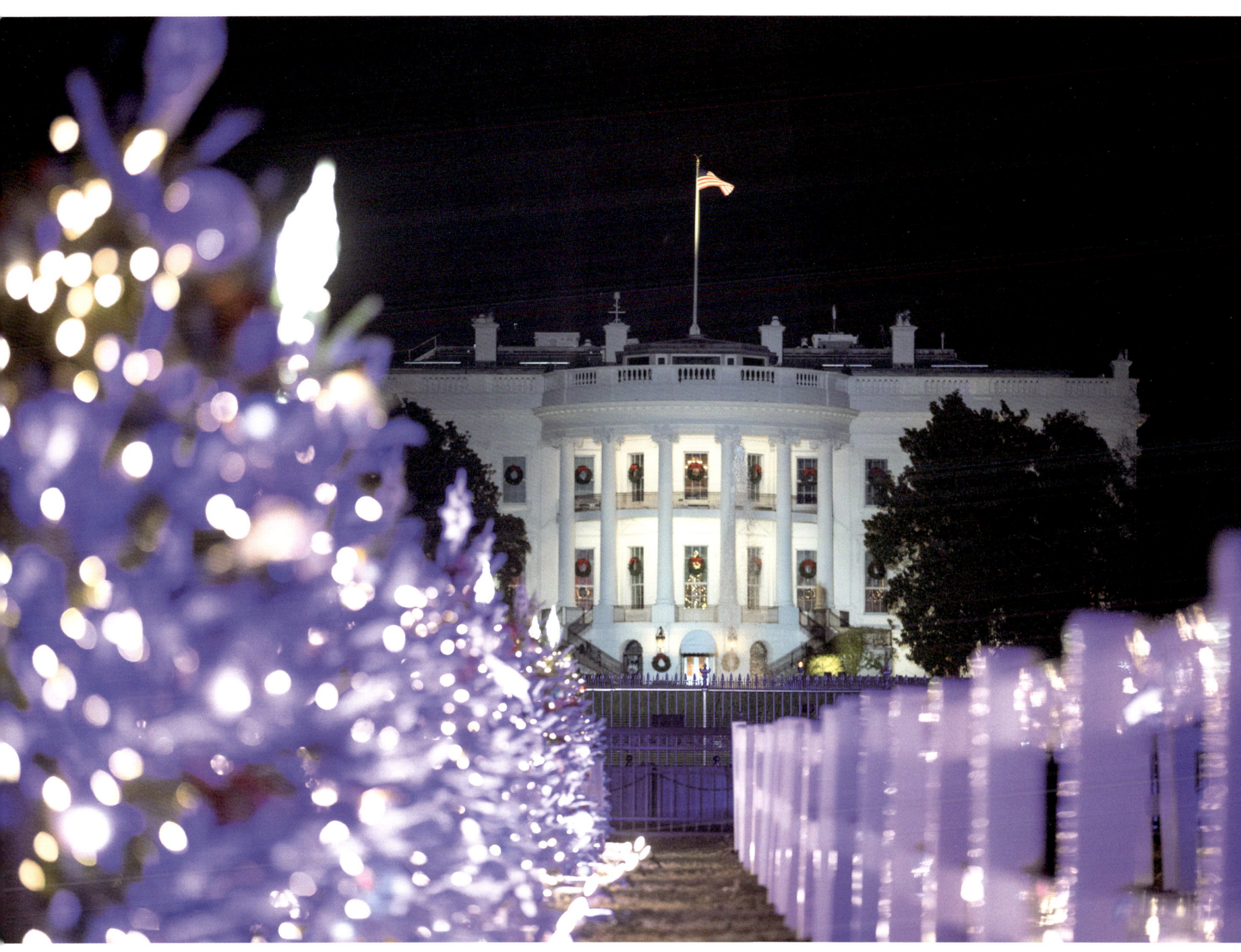

The South Portico of the White House is framed in Christmas lights during the Lighting of the National Christmas Tree festivities on the Ellipse in Washington, D.C. (Official White House Photo by Joyce N. Boghosian)

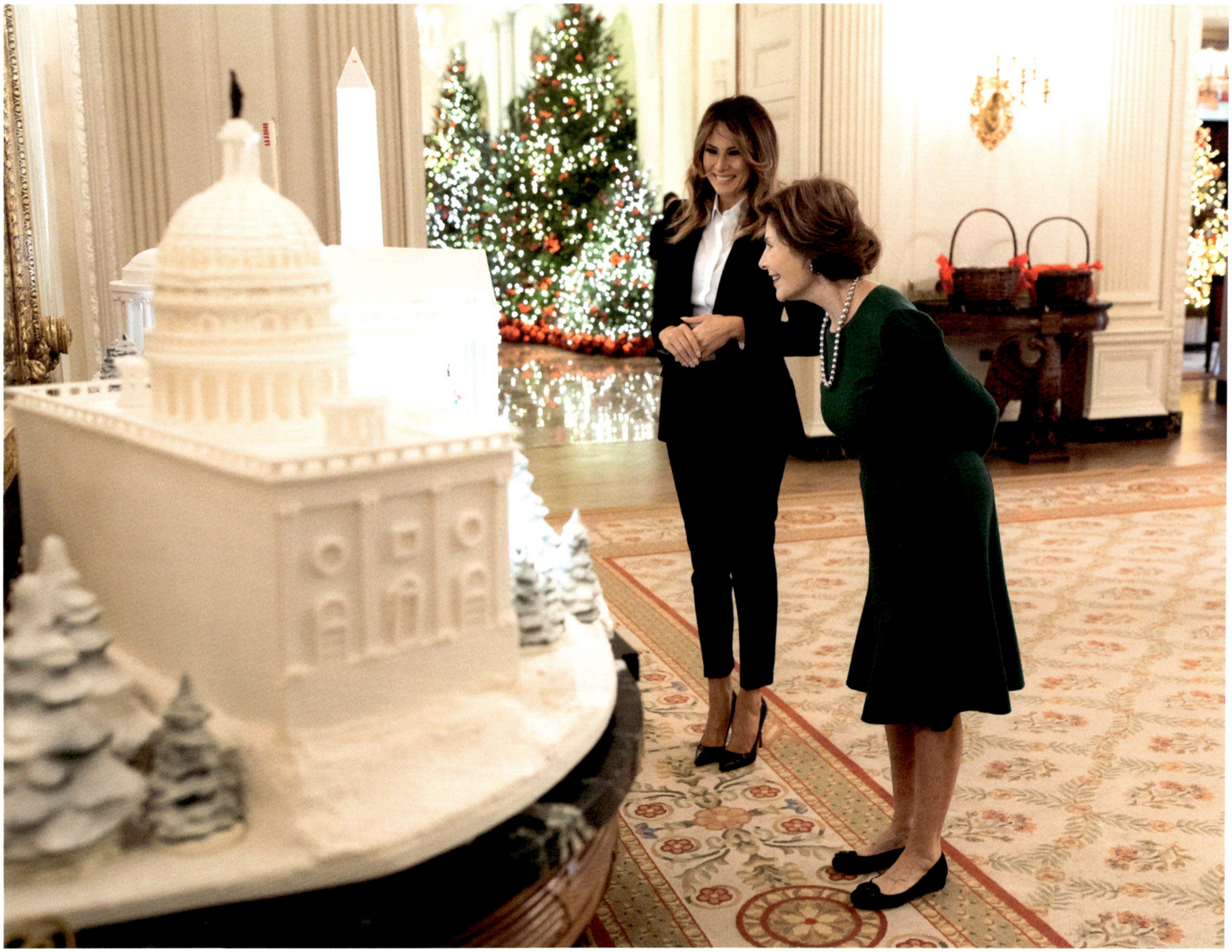

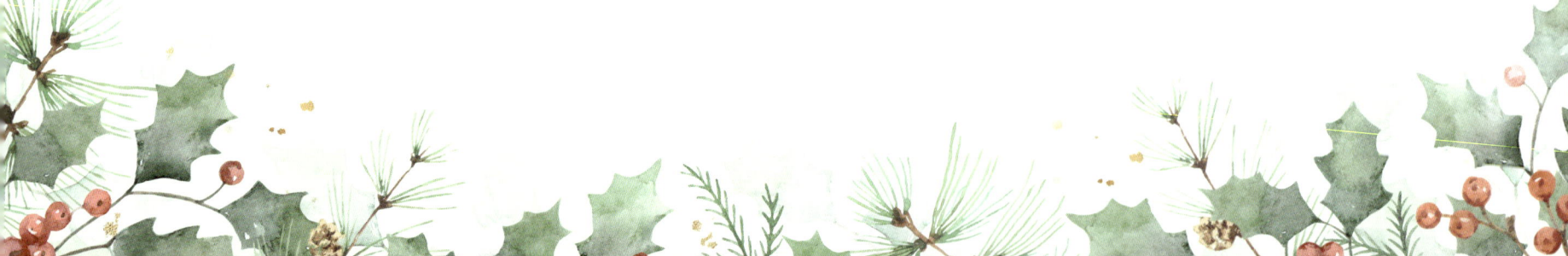

First Lady Melania Trump shows former First Lady Laura Bush the gingerbread house during a Christmas tour in the State Dining Room of the White House.

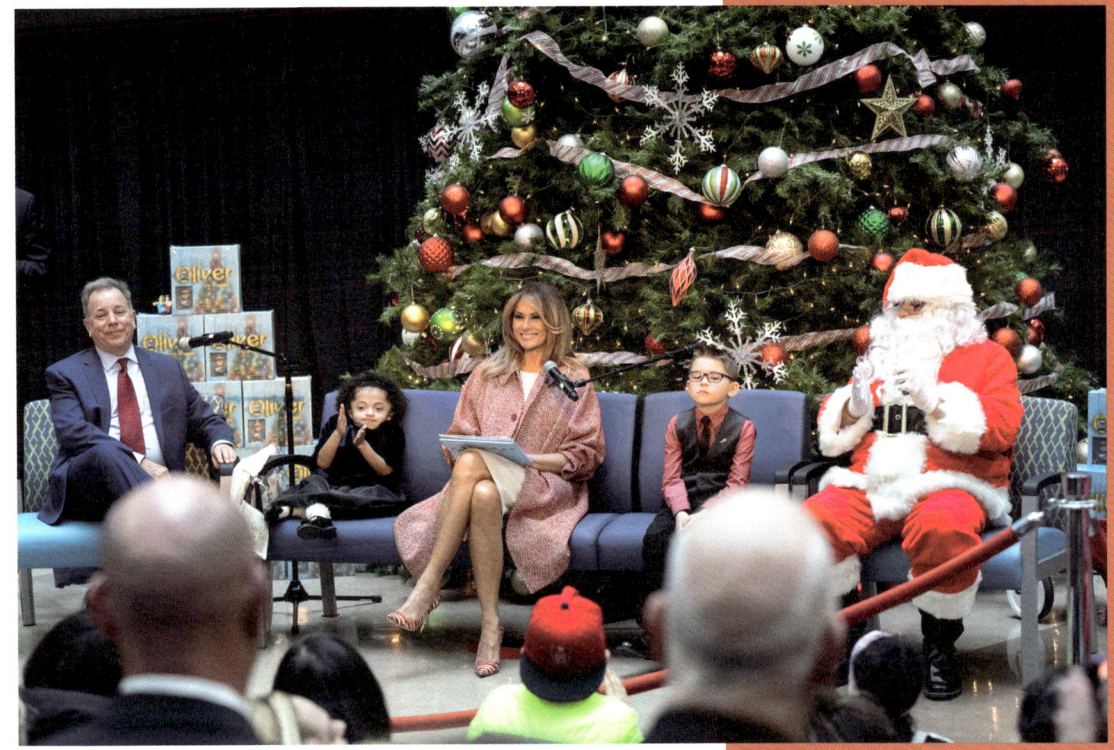

First Lady Melania Trump reads *Oliver the Ornament* to children and families at Children's National Hospital in Washington, D.C.

First Lady Melania Trump greets patients and their families at Children's National Hospital in Washington, D.C.

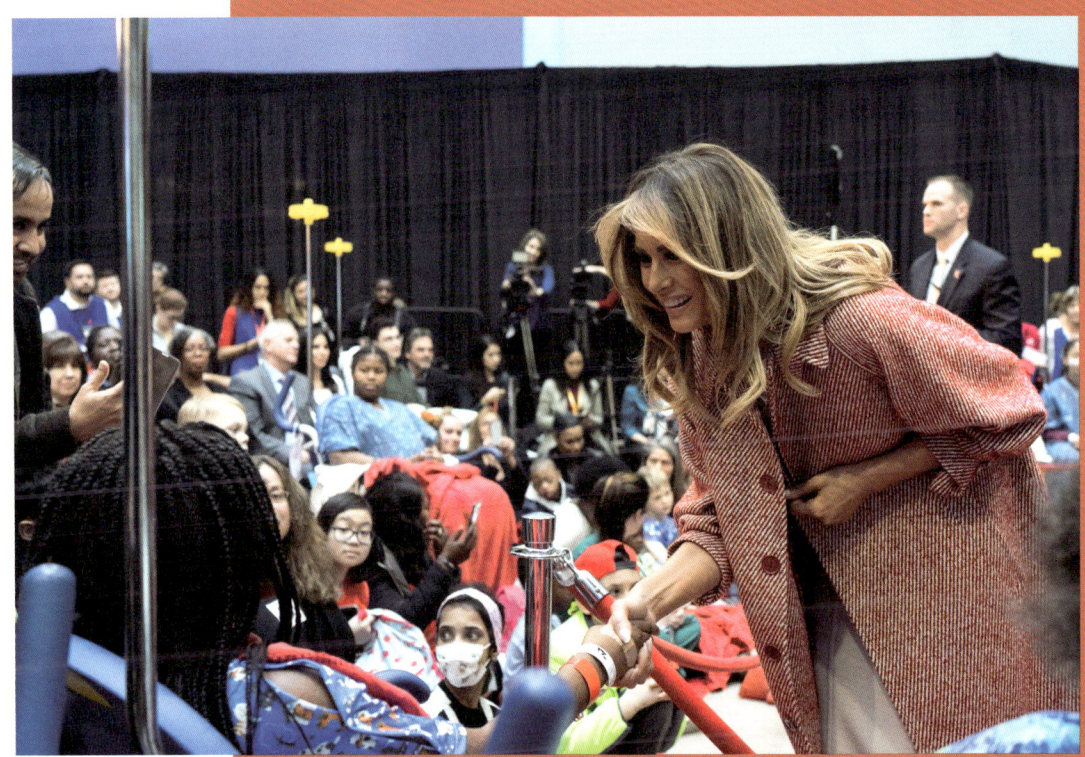

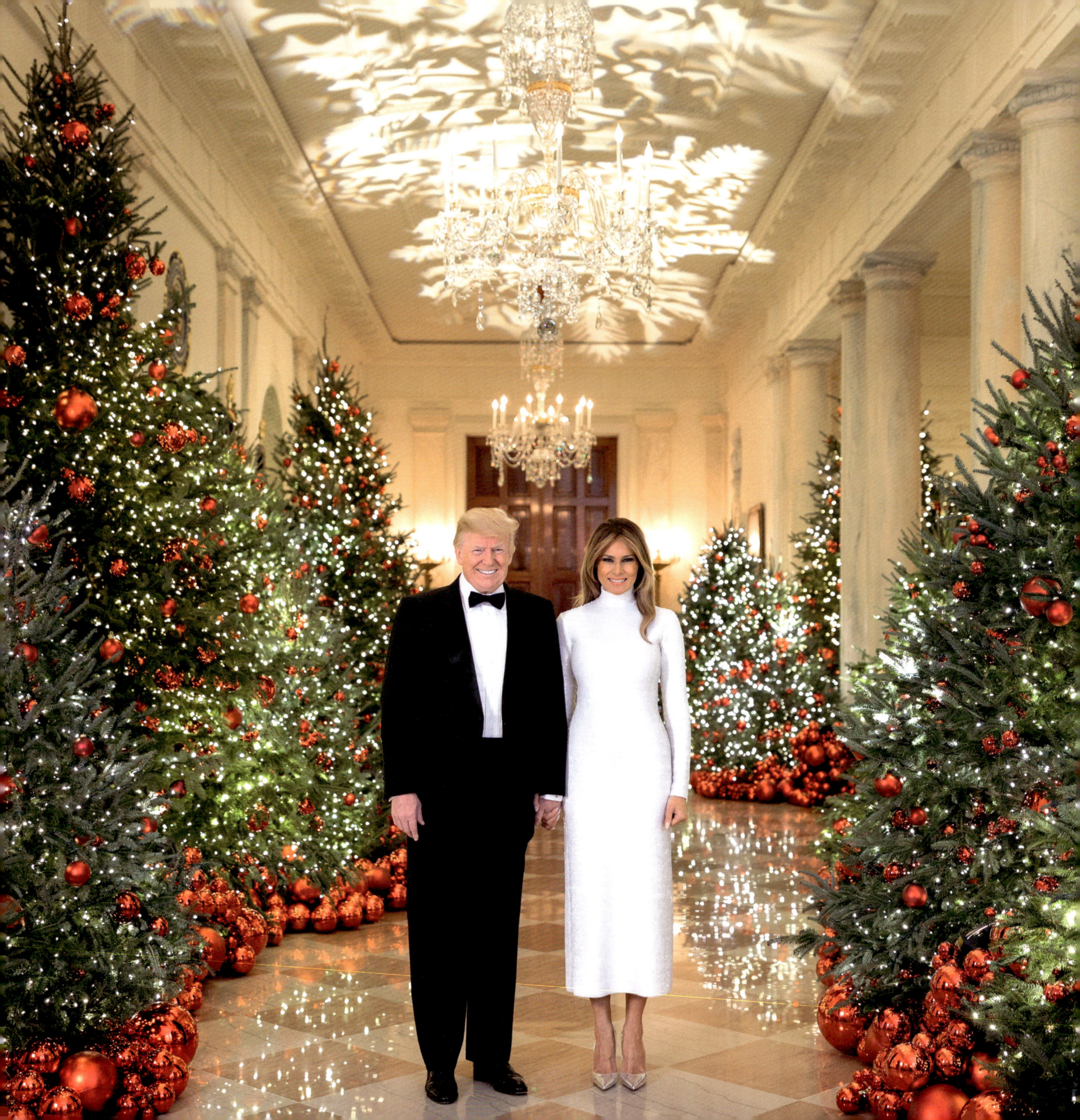

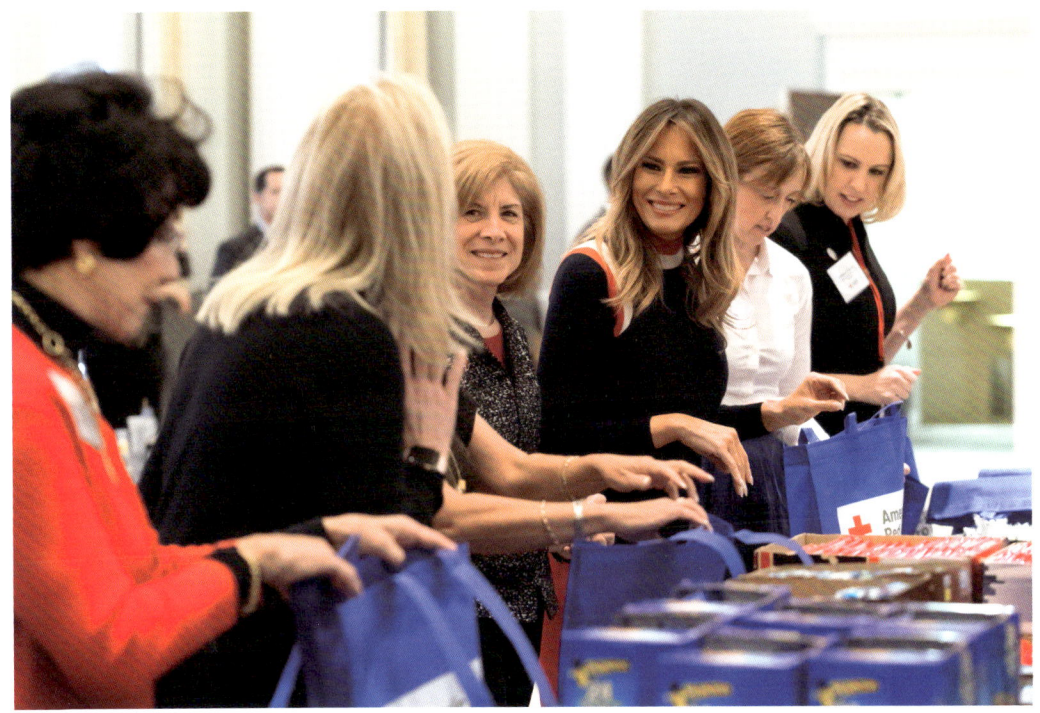

First Lady Melania Trump helps volunteers assemble military comfort kits for deployed American troops at the American Red Cross Headquarters in Washington, D.C.

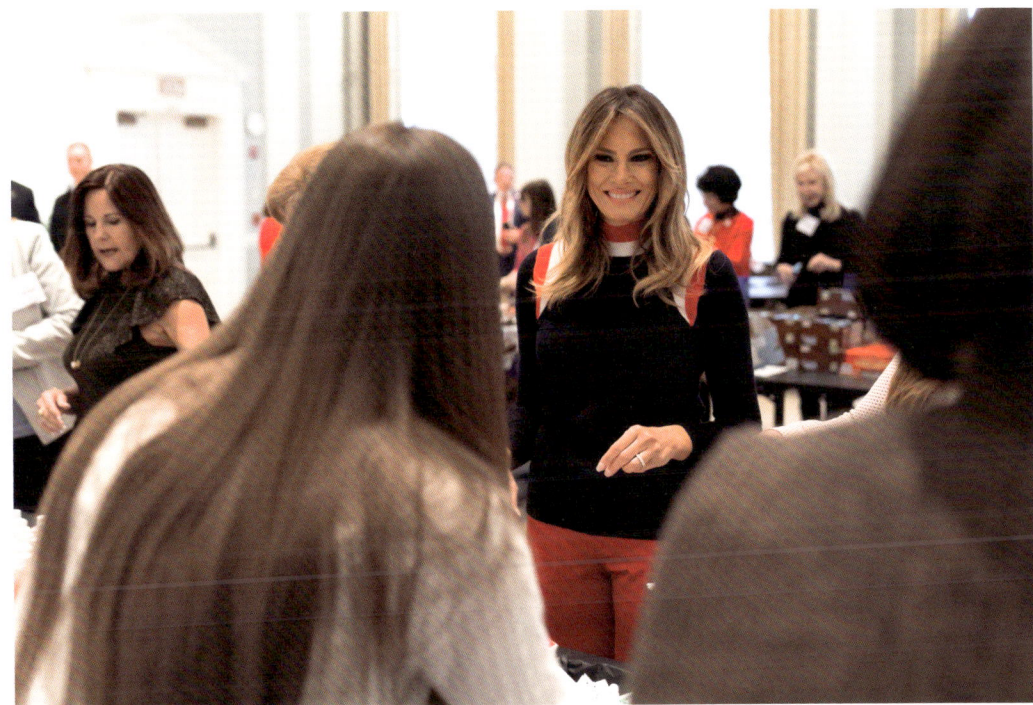

Second Lady Karen Pence joins the First Lady to help assembly military comfort kits with the American Red Cross.

Left: The President and First Lady are seen in their Official Christmas Portrait in the Cross Hall of the White House.

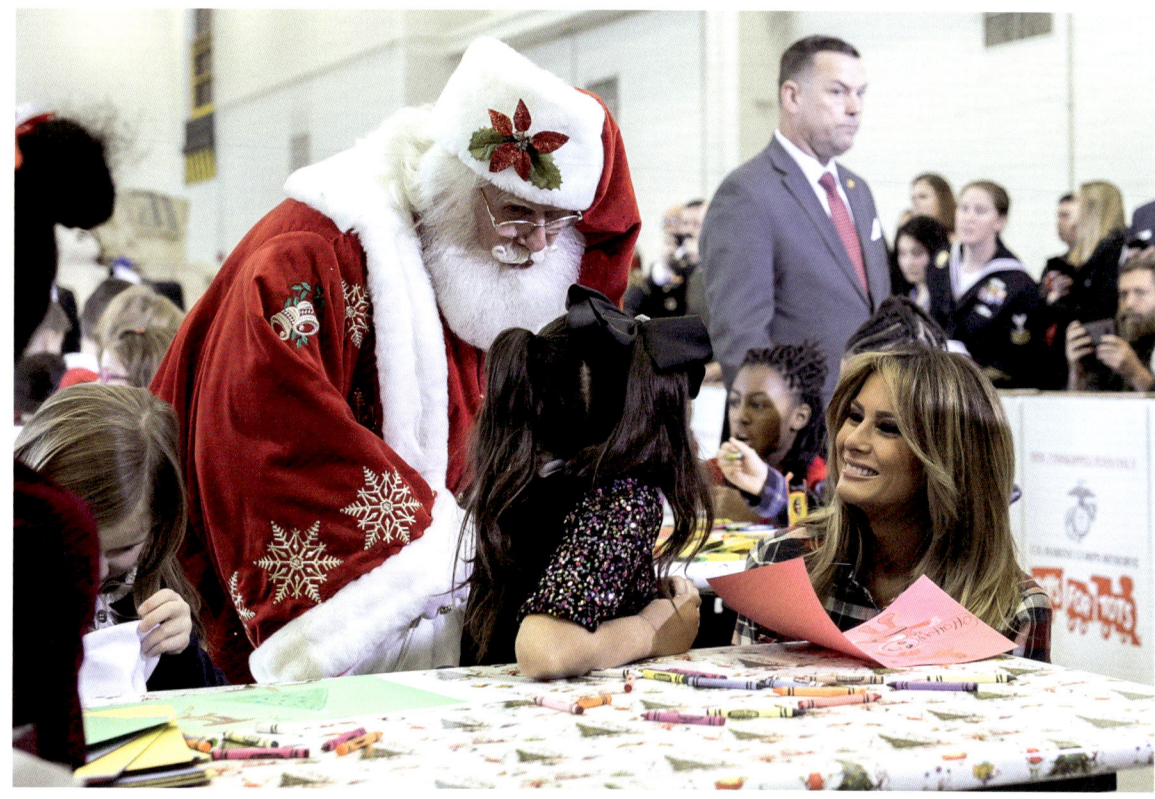

The First Lady and Santa Claus spread holiday cheer to the children at the Toys for Tots Christmas Event at Joint Base Anacostia-Bolling.

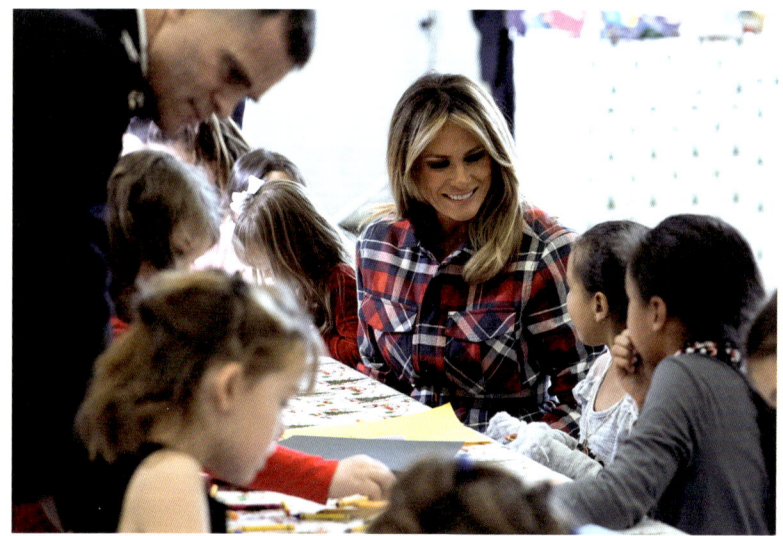

The First Lady meets with children for a second year at the Toys for Tots Christmas Event at Joint Base Anacostia-Bolling in Washington, D.C.

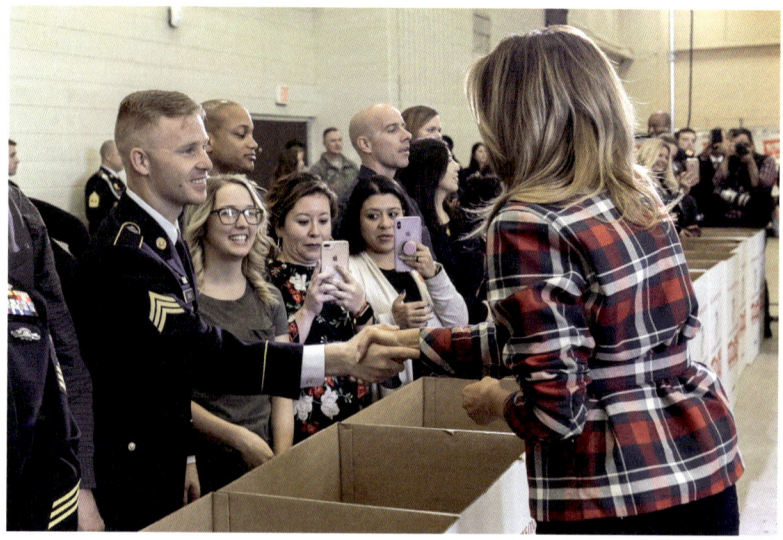

First Lady Melania Trump shakes hands with guests at the Toys for Tots Christmas Event at Joint Base Anacostia-Bolling.

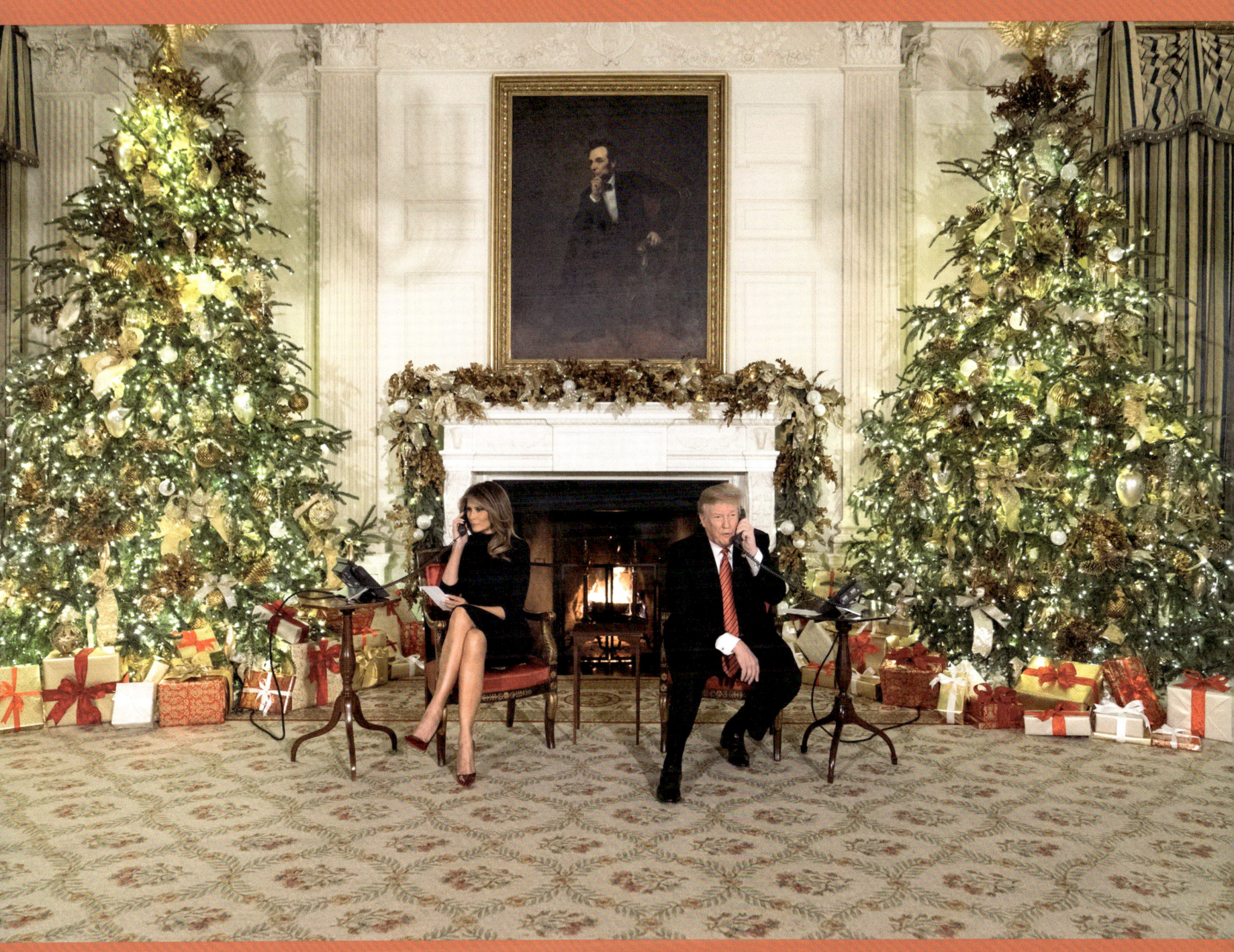

President Trump and First Lady Melania Trump participate in NORAD Santa Tracker phone calls on Christmas Eve in the State Dining Room of the White House—a Christmas Eve tradition for over 60 years that helps to keep track of Santa's travels around the world. (Official White House Photo by Shealah Craighead)

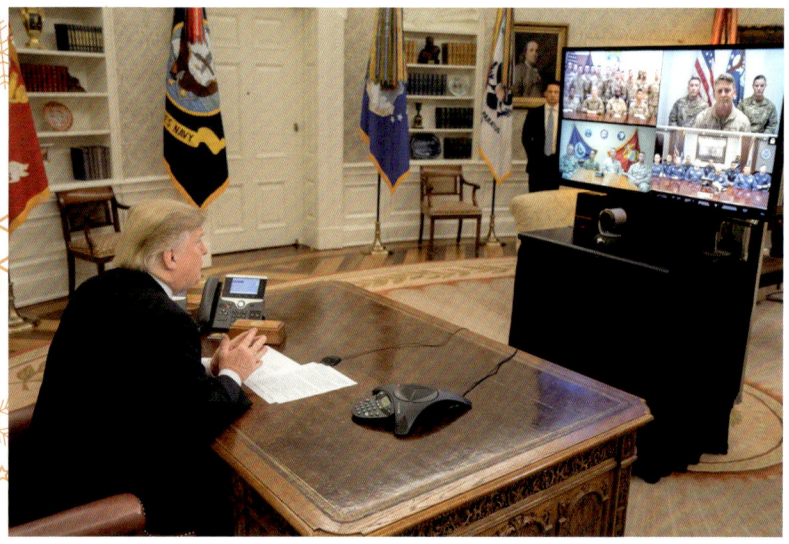

President Donald J. Trump participates in a video conference from the Oval Office on Christmas Day, speaking with military service members stationed at remote sites worldwide to thank them for their service to our nation. (Official White House Photo by Shealah Craighead)

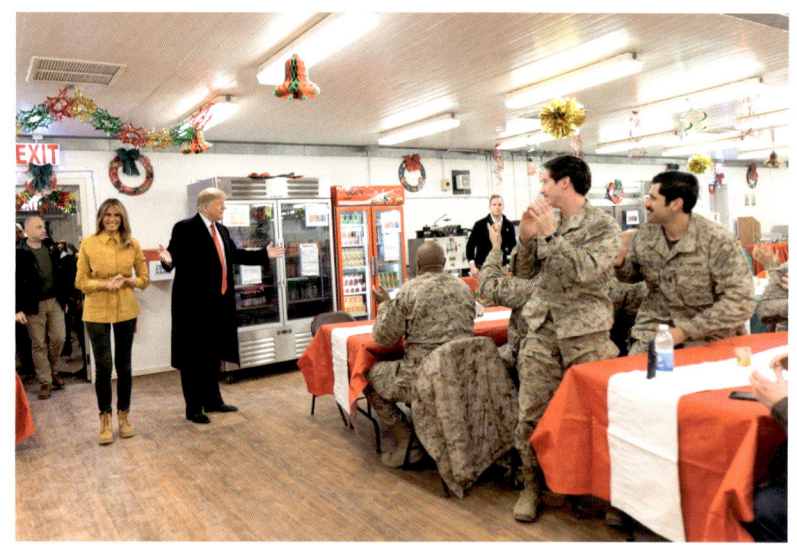

President Donald J. Trump, joined by First Lady Melania Trump, visits U.S. troops at their dining hall Wednesday, December 26, 2018, at the Al-Asad Airbase in Iraq. (Official White House Photo by Shealah Craighead)

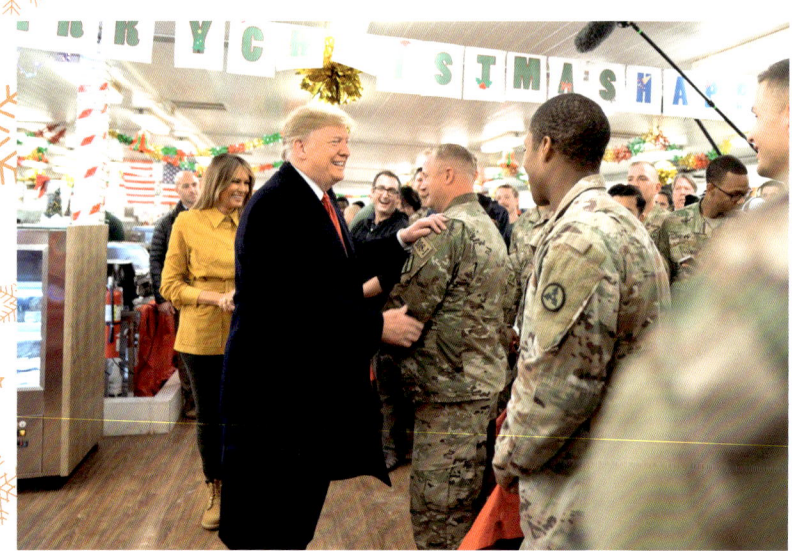

The President and First Lady spend the day after Christmas shaking hands and speaking with U.S. troops at the Al-Asad Airbase in Iraq. (Official White House Photo by Shealah Craighead)

"@FLOTUS Melania and I were honored to visit our incredible troops at Al-Asad Air Base in Iraq. GOD BLESS THE U.S.A.!"

—President Donald J. Trump, 2018

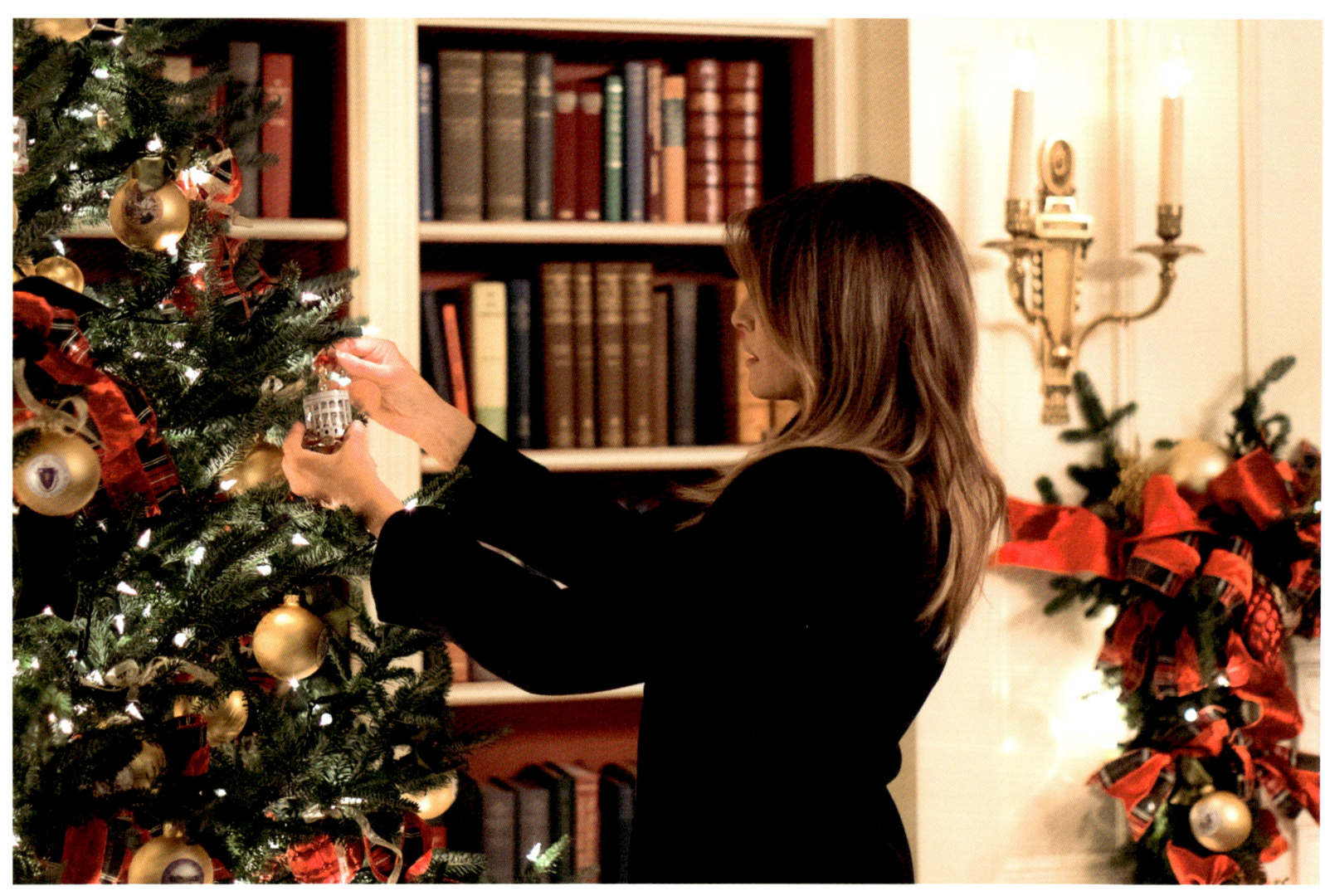

Melania Trump hangs the Official 2018 White House Christmas Ornament in the Library of the White House.

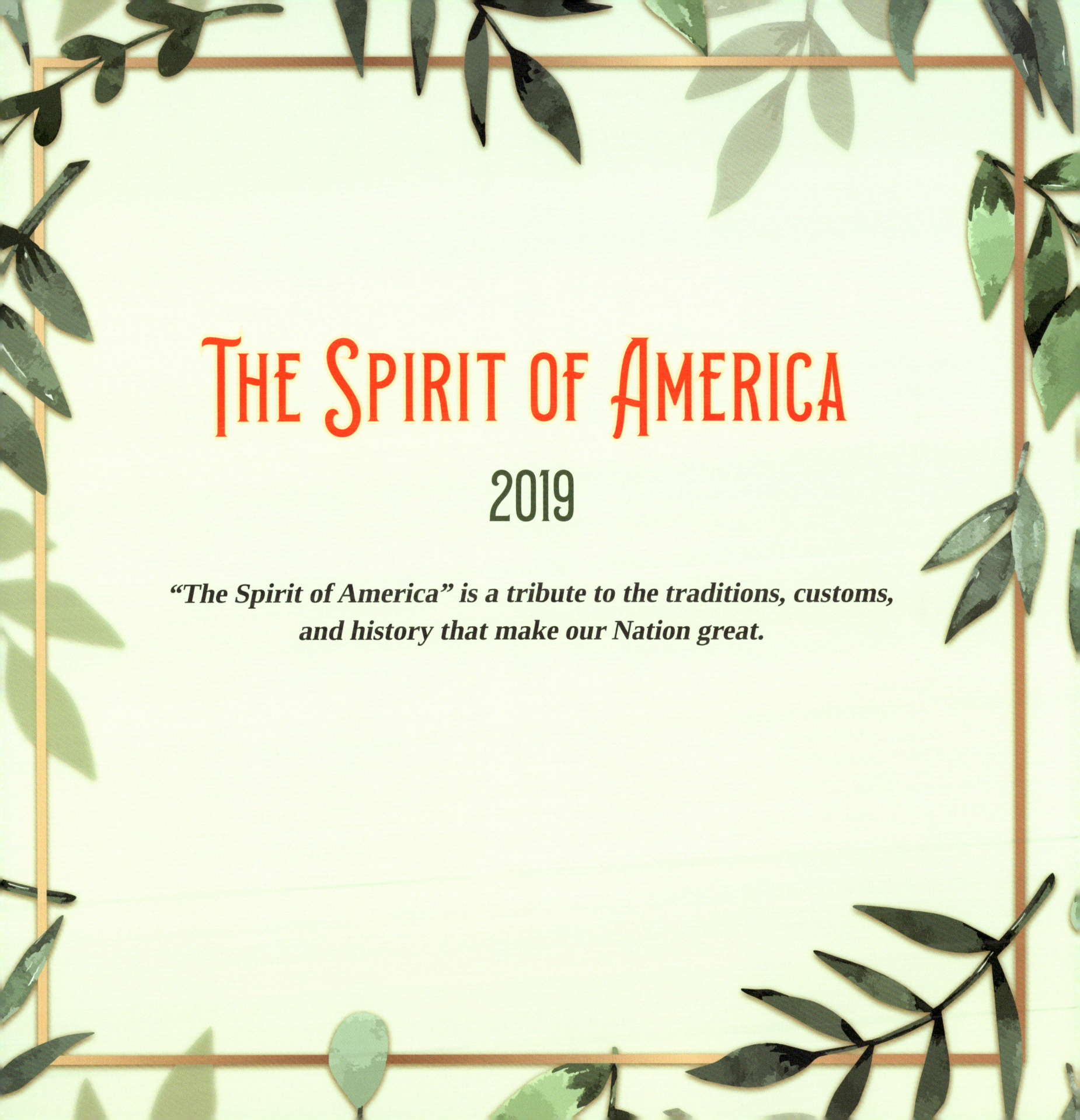

The Spirit of America

2019

"The Spirit of America" is a tribute to the traditions, customs, and history that make our Nation great.

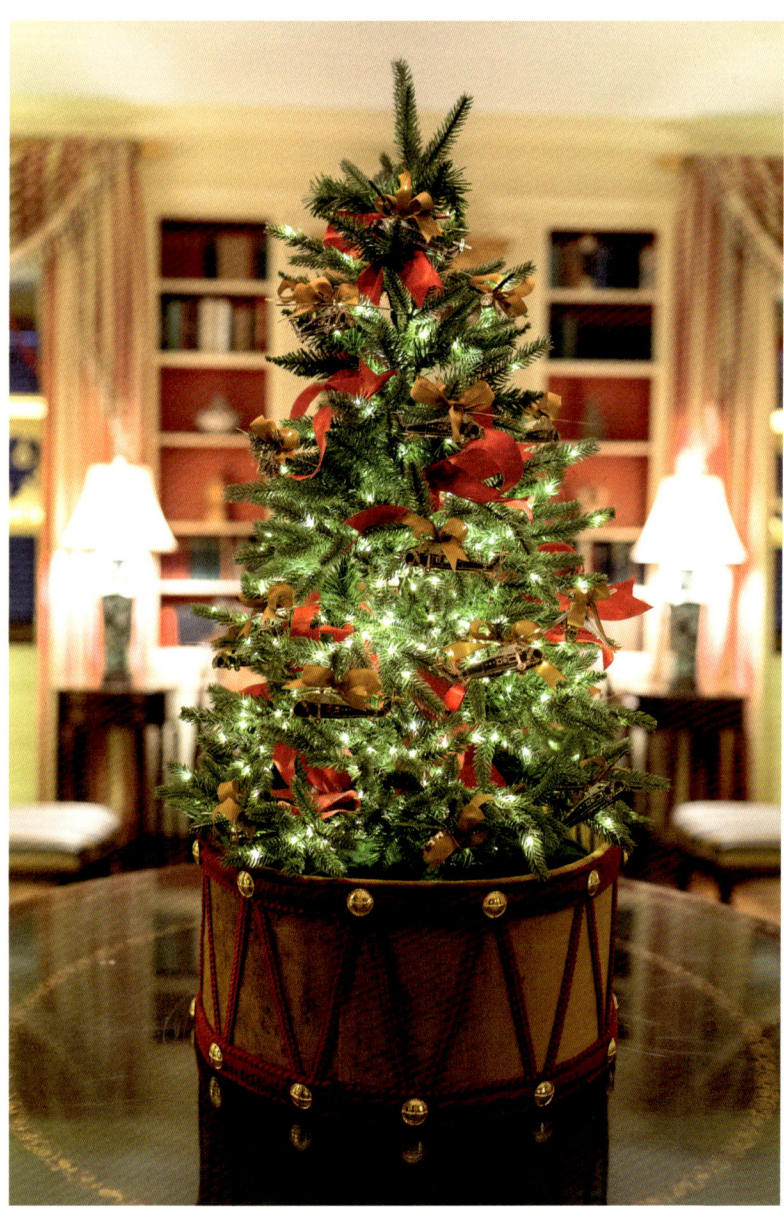

The 2019 White House Christmas Ornament is seen decorating a tree in the Library of the White House.

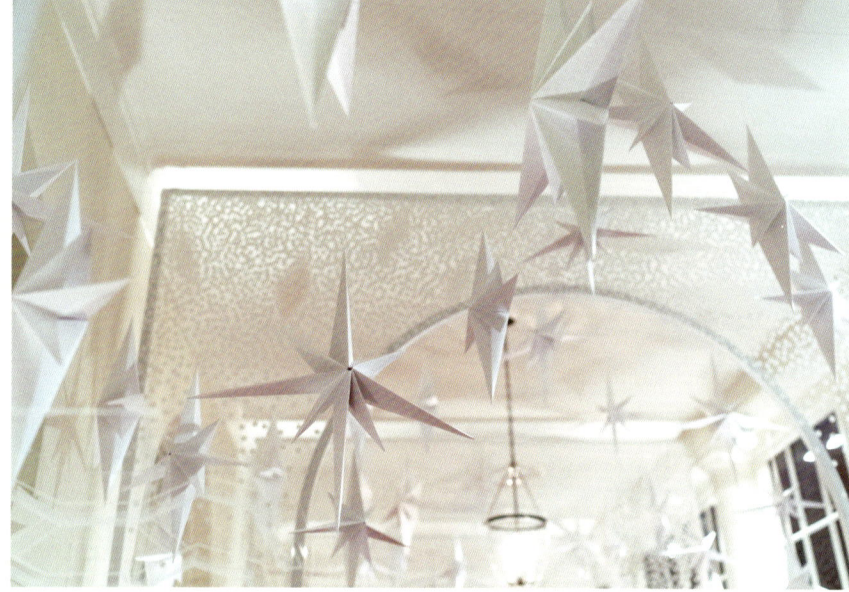

The ceiling of the East Wing Colonnade is decorated with a canopy of wintery, white stars.

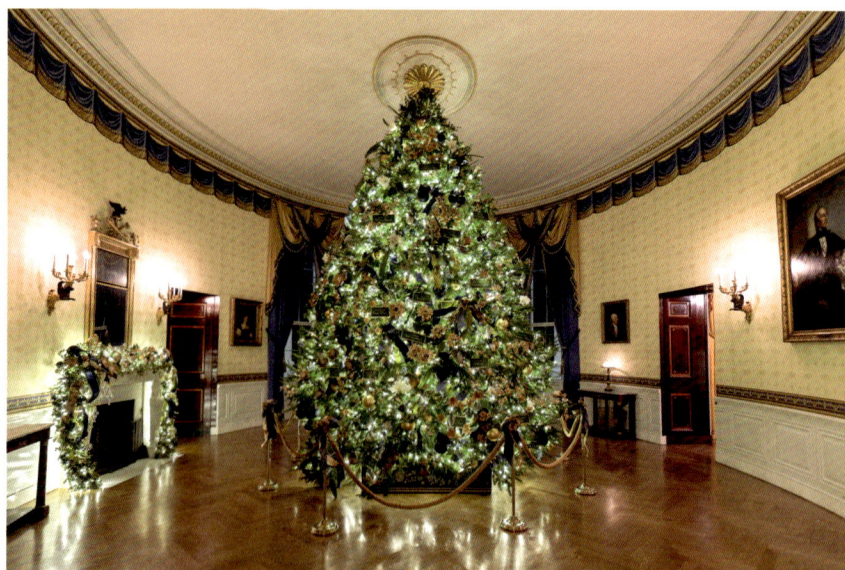

The Official Christmas Tree in the Blue Room is covered with paper flowers representing each of the states' official flowers, signaling the diversity of our country.

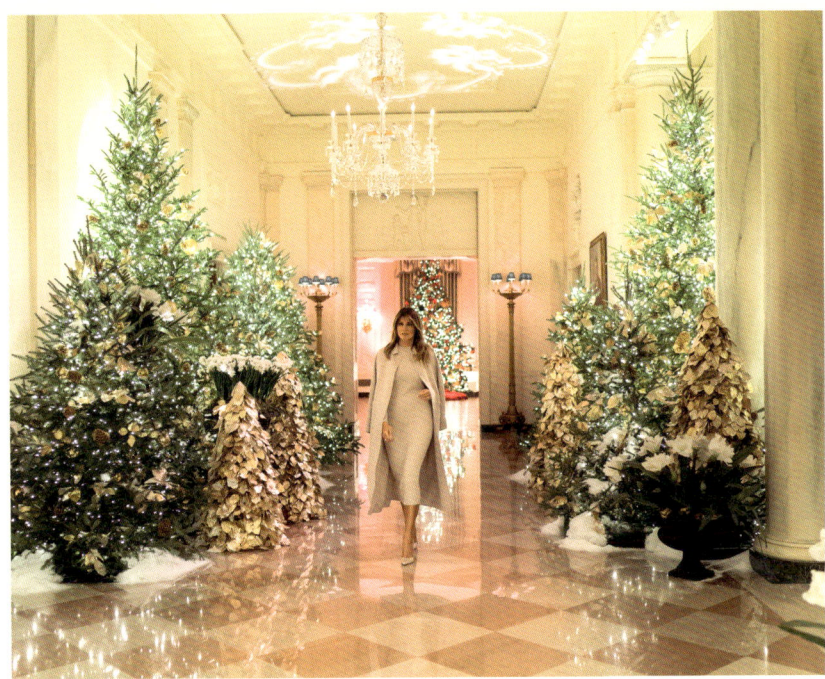

The First Lady surveys Christmas decorations in the Cross Hall of the White House.

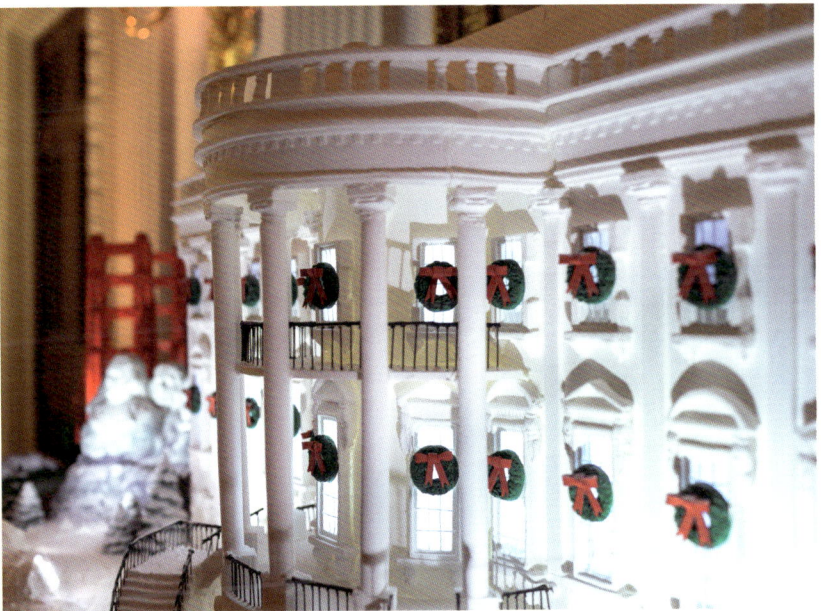

The Gingerbread House is displayed in the State Dining Room of the White House for the Christmas season. This year it features landmarks from across the country alongside the White House.

In the East Colonnade there was a timeline of American design, innovation and architecture. Through the archways, the East Garden Room displayed the First Family's annual ornament and Christmas card. In 2019, both displayed the American flag symbolizing the United States' pride. The Vermeil Room honored the spirit of generosity of previous First Ladies. Two trees were illuminated with blush and gold hues and pieces of historic vermeil. The 2019 ornament was displayed in the library and paid tribute to Dwight D. Eisenhower. The China Room was set with a holiday feast, illustrating a family coming together during the holidays and sharing in the Christmas spirit.

The East Room shone with four star-spangled trees that reached for the ceiling, glimmering with stars and cascading ribbons. At the top of each tree was a golden eagle, representing freedom and strength. The American flag was incorporated into the decorations: red symbolizes bravery and valor, and blue glows with perseverance and justice. The 2019 gingerbread house was created to represent the South Portico of the White House and landmarks across the country: the Golden Gate Bridge, Space Needle, Mount Rushmore, the Alamo, Gateway Arch, Liberty Bell, and the Statue of Liberty. The White House pastry team constructed the tremendous masterpiece out of 200 lbs. of gingerbread dough, 125 lbs. of pastillage dough, 35 lbs. of chocolate, and 25 lbs. of royal icing!

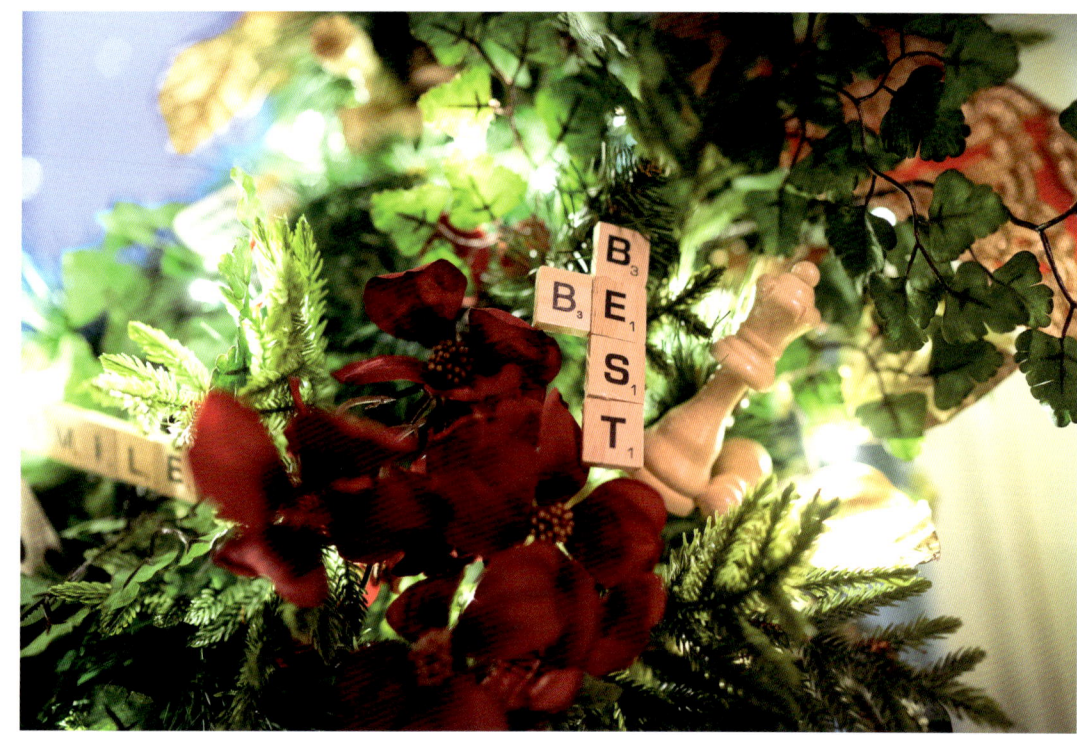

The Red Room of the White House is decorated with games and toys to highlight the childlike wonder of the holiday season. The First Lady's BE BEST initiative is featured in the decorations.

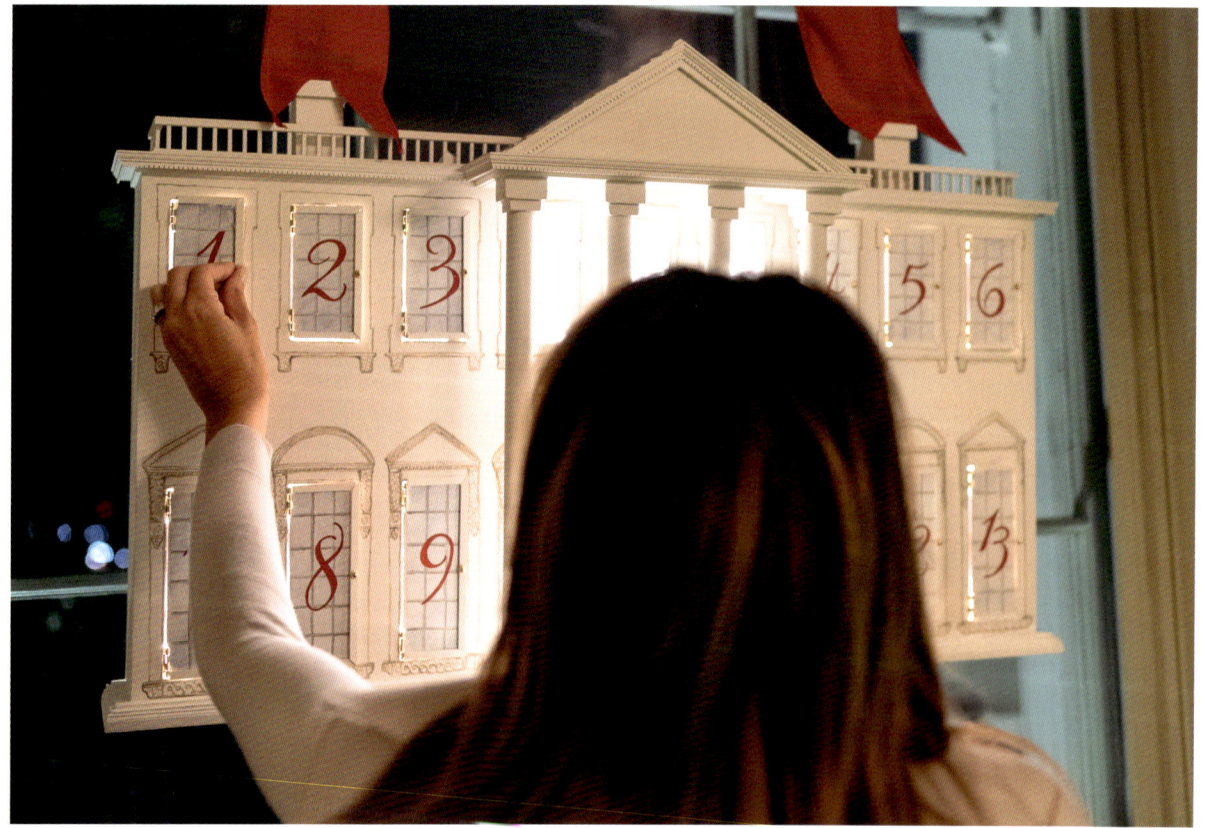

First Lady Melania Trump looks at an advent calendar in the Green Room of the White House.

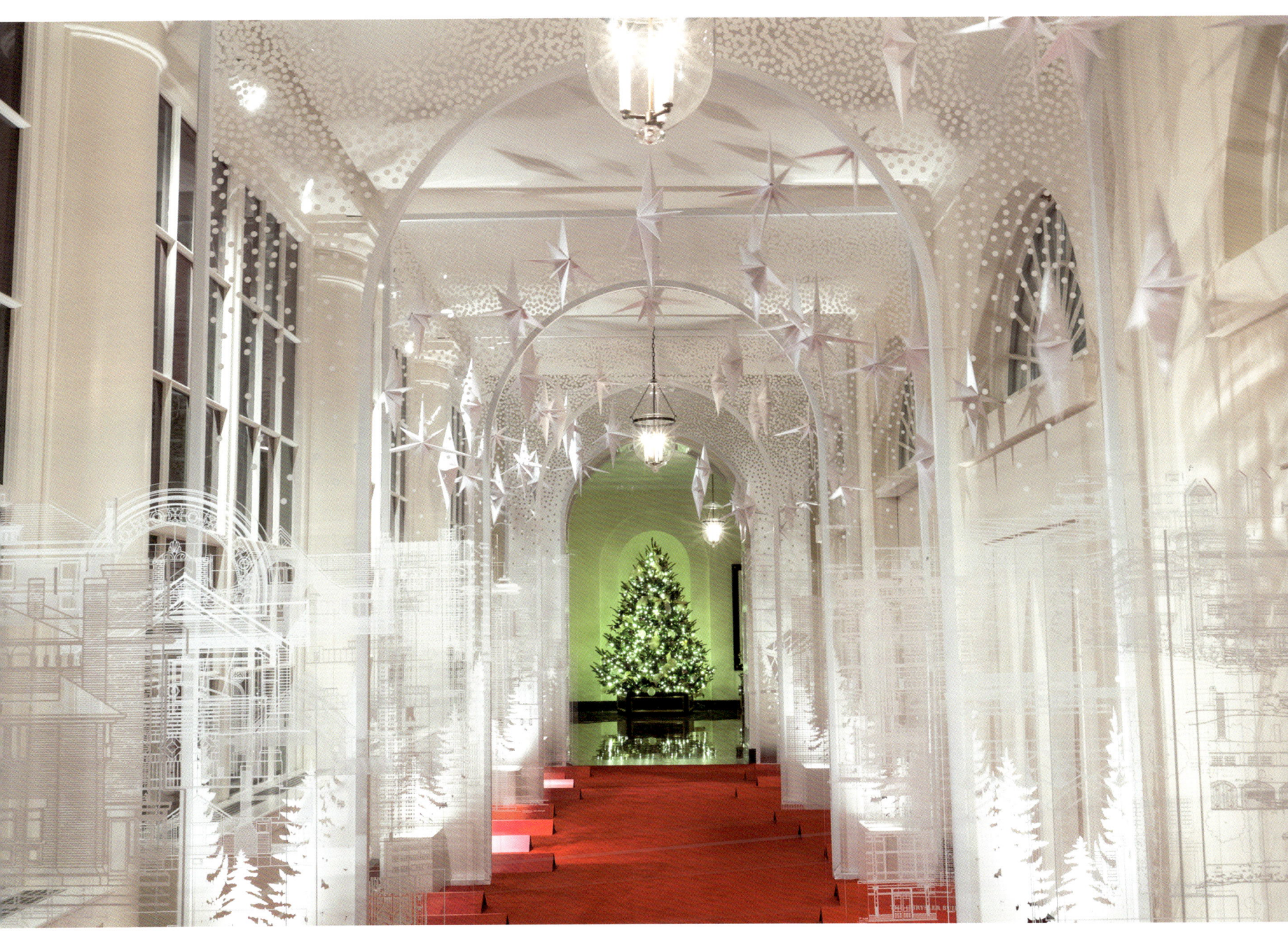

The East Wing Colonnade of the White House is seen decorated for the Christmas season. This year the decorations highlight American innovations in design and architecture from America's founding to the modern day.

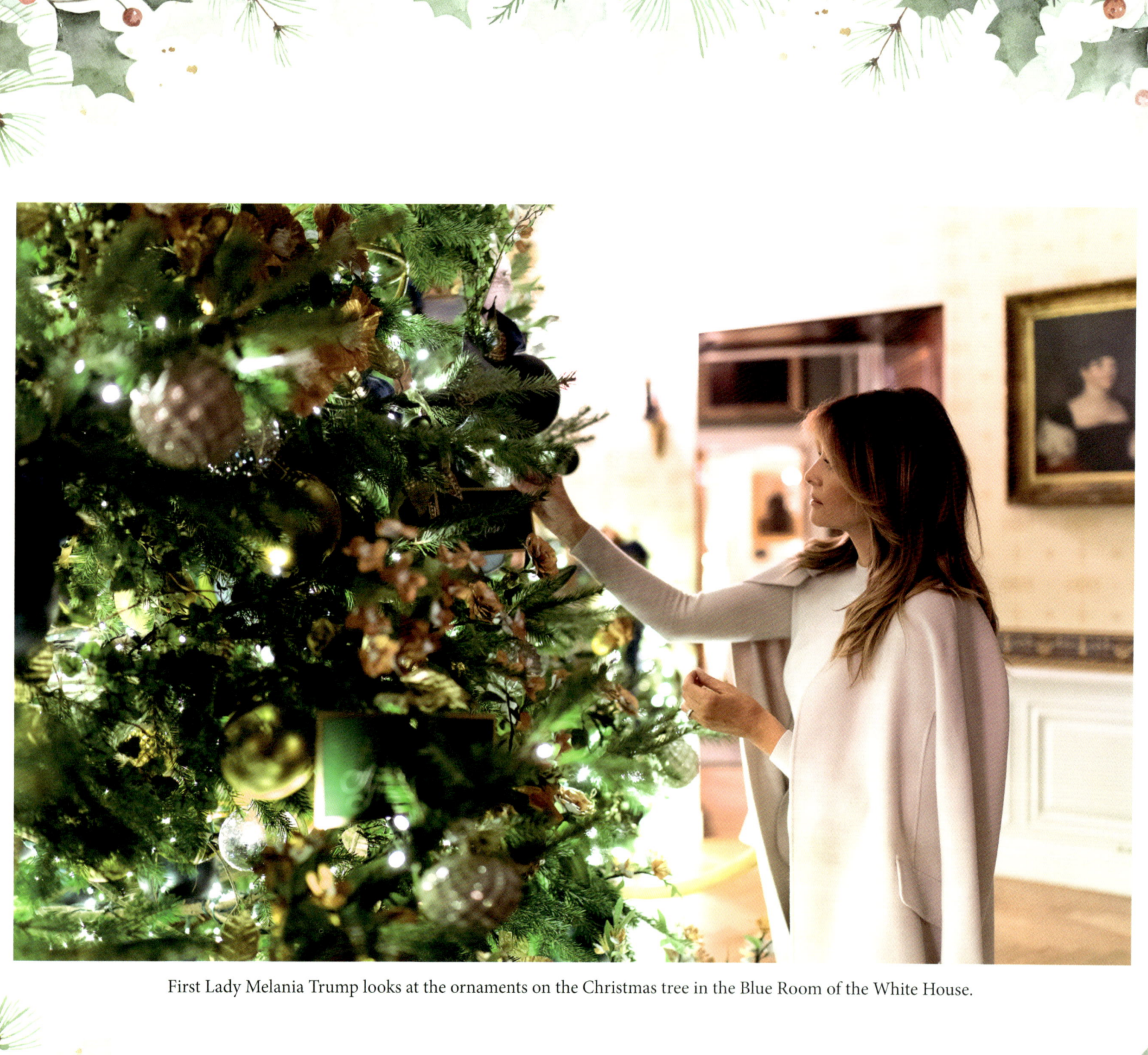

First Lady Melania Trump looks at the ornaments on the Christmas tree in the Blue Room of the White House.

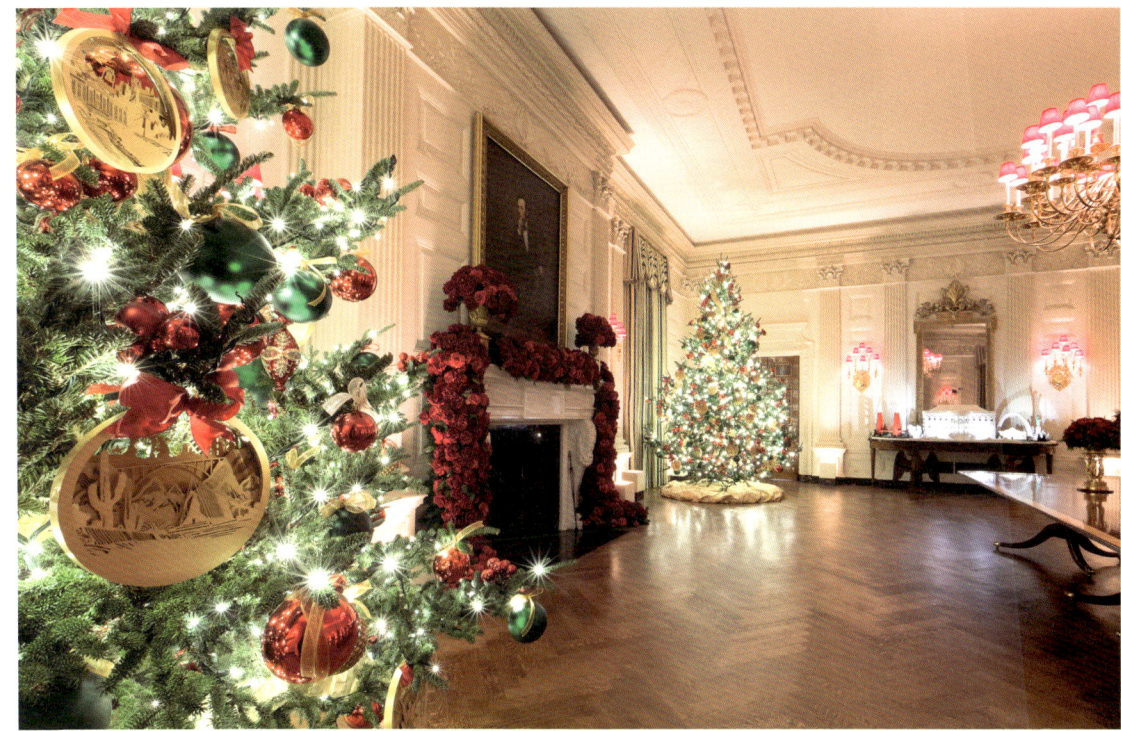

The decor of the State Dining Room of the White House celebrates the diversity of our fifty states and showcases the official Gingerbread House.

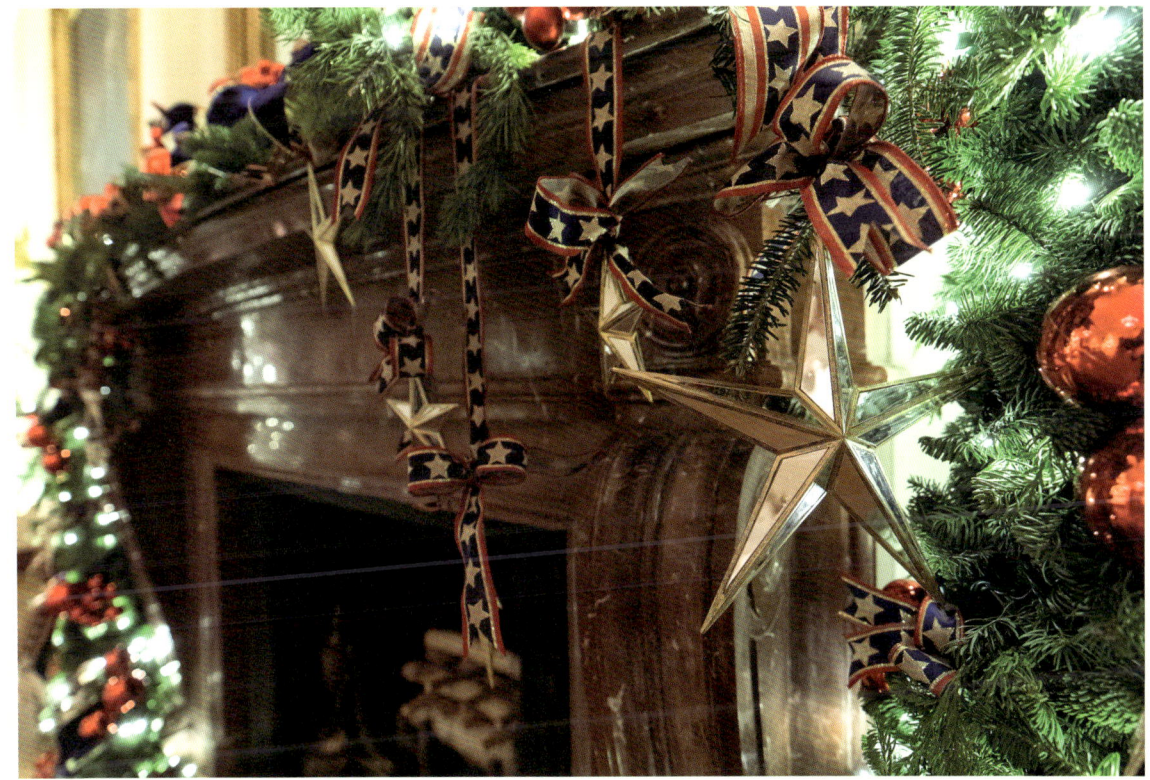

The mantles in the East Room are decorated with stars and stripes, honoring the American Flag.

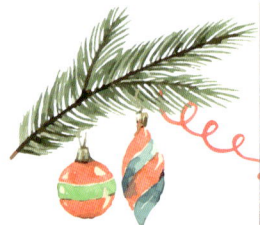

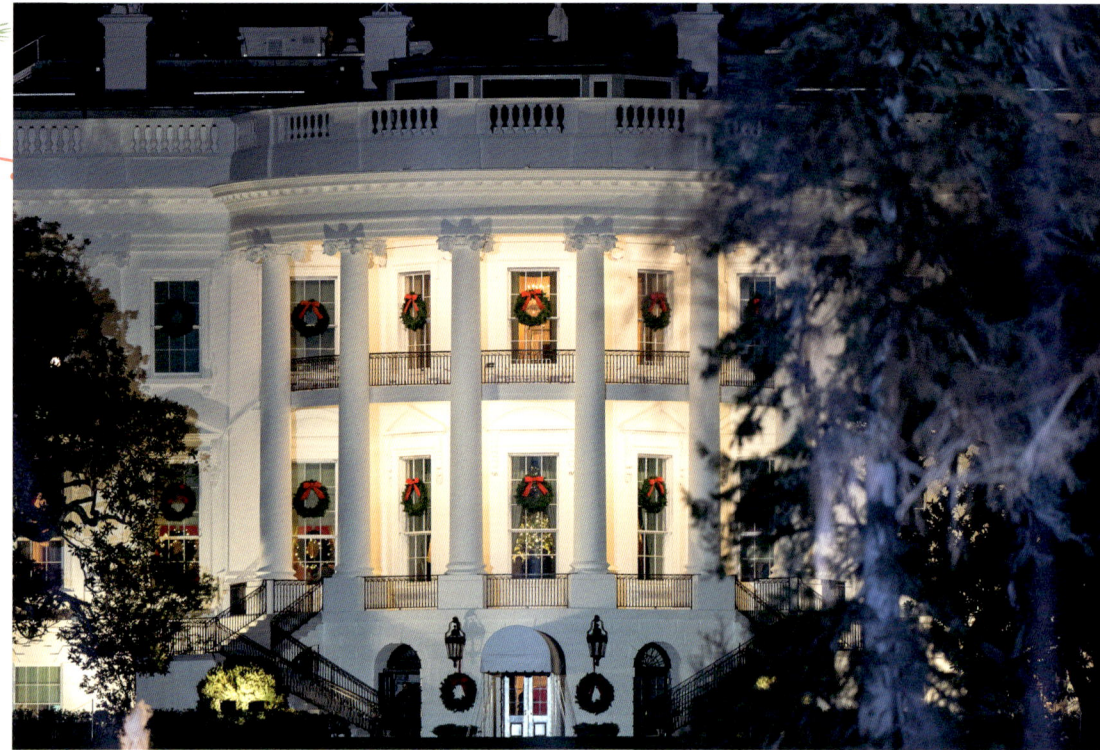

The South Portico is decorated with the First Lady's traditional wreaths and lit up for the Christmas holiday. (Official White House Photo by Joyce N. Boghosian)

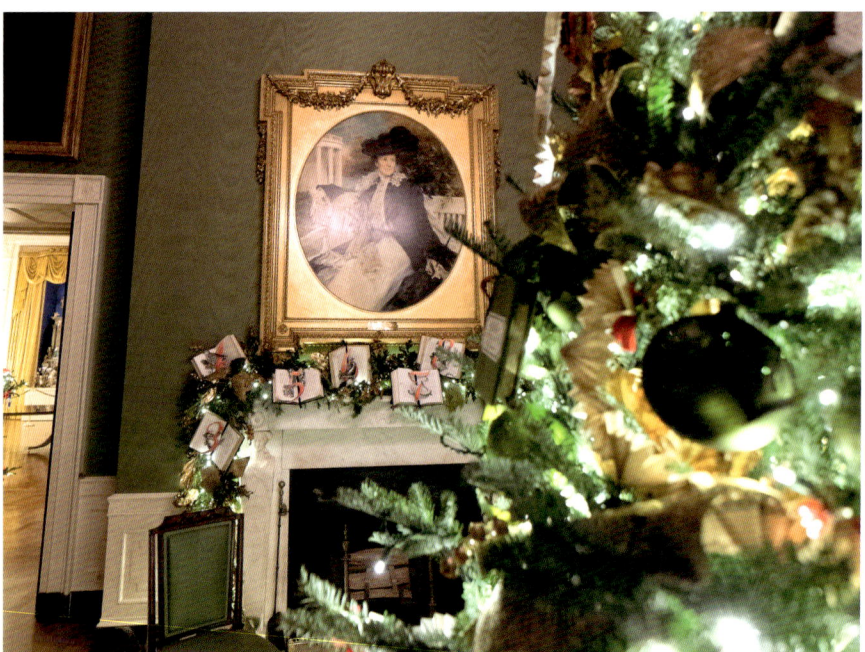

The Green Room of the White House celebrates traditional Christmas stories, the mantle decorated with books highlighting the Twelve Days of Christmas.

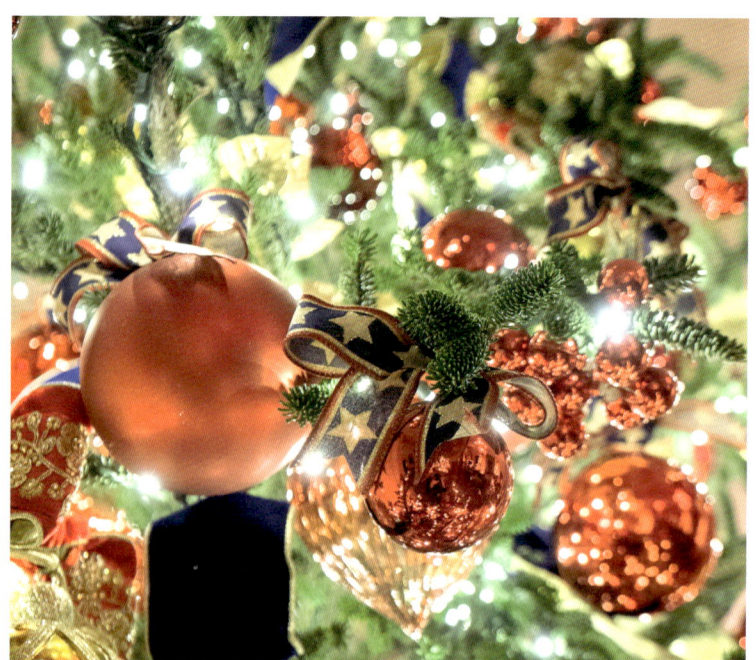

The trees in the East Room are decorated with red ornaments for bravery and blue ribbons for perseverance, symbolizing American Patriotism.

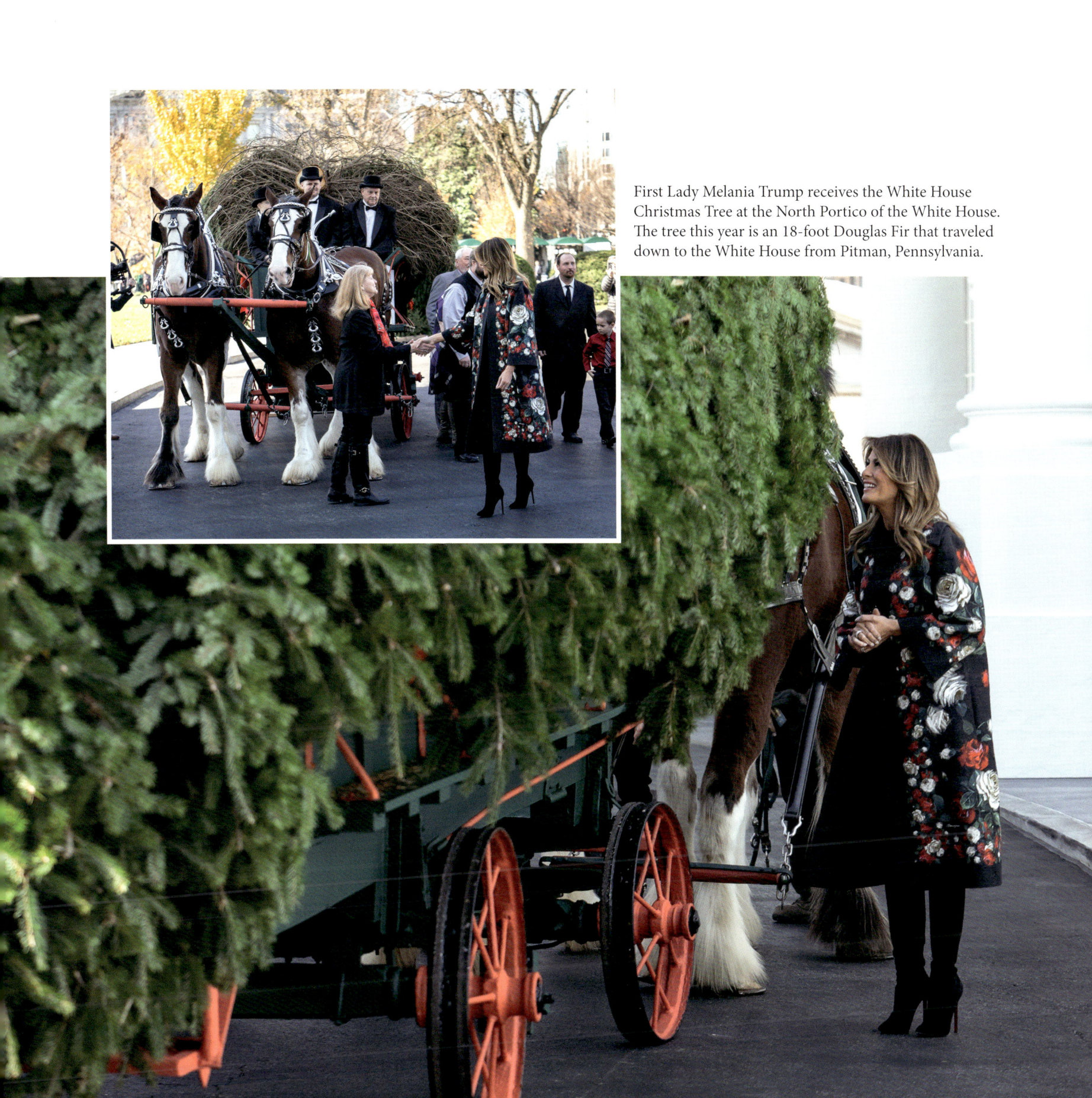

First Lady Melania Trump receives the White House Christmas Tree at the North Portico of the White House. The tree this year is an 18-foot Douglas Fir that traveled down to the White House from Pitman, Pennsylvania.

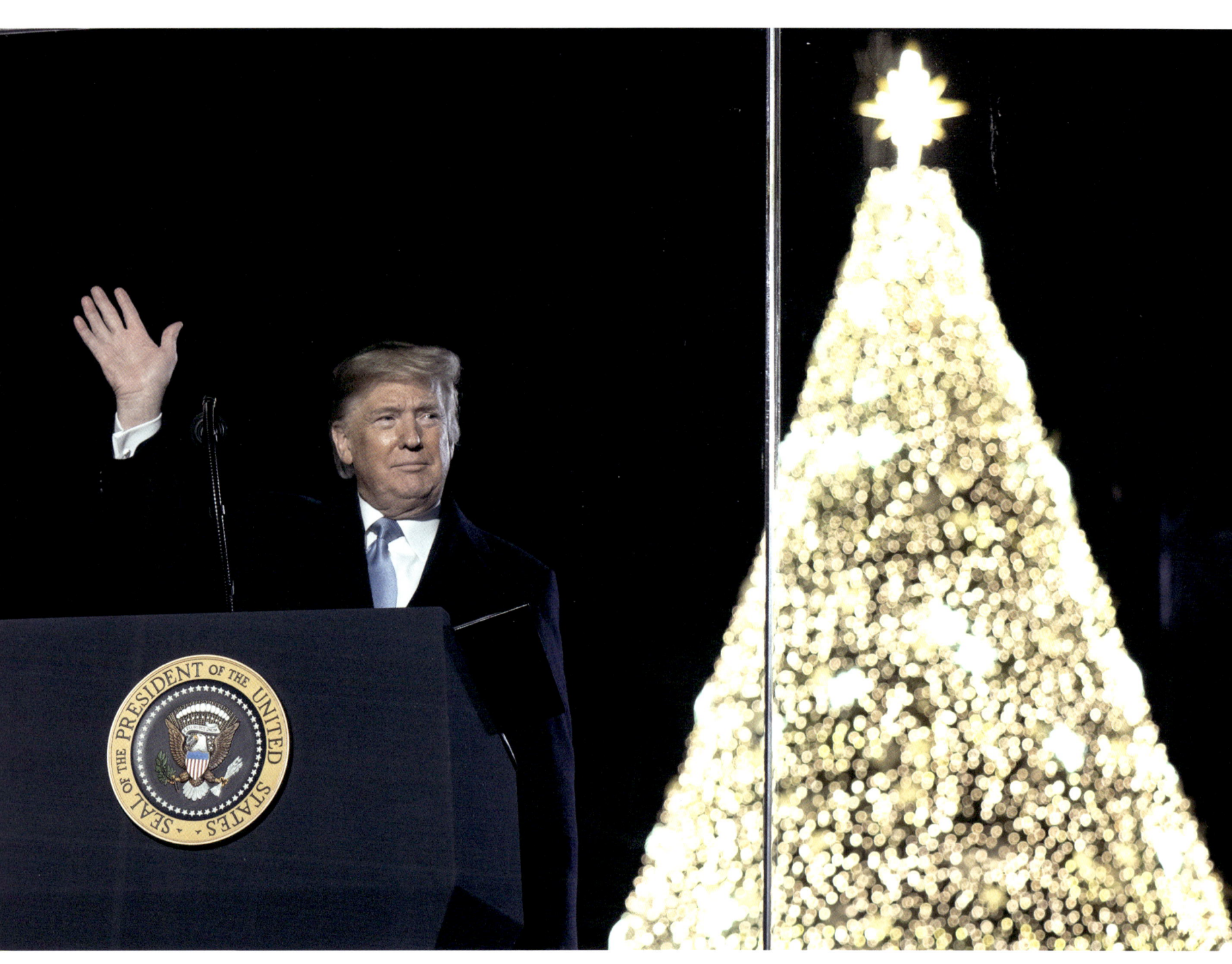

President Donald J. Trump waves to the crowd at the National Christmas Tree Lighting 2019 ceremony on the Ellipse in Washington, D.C. (Official White House Photo by Joyce N. Boghosian)

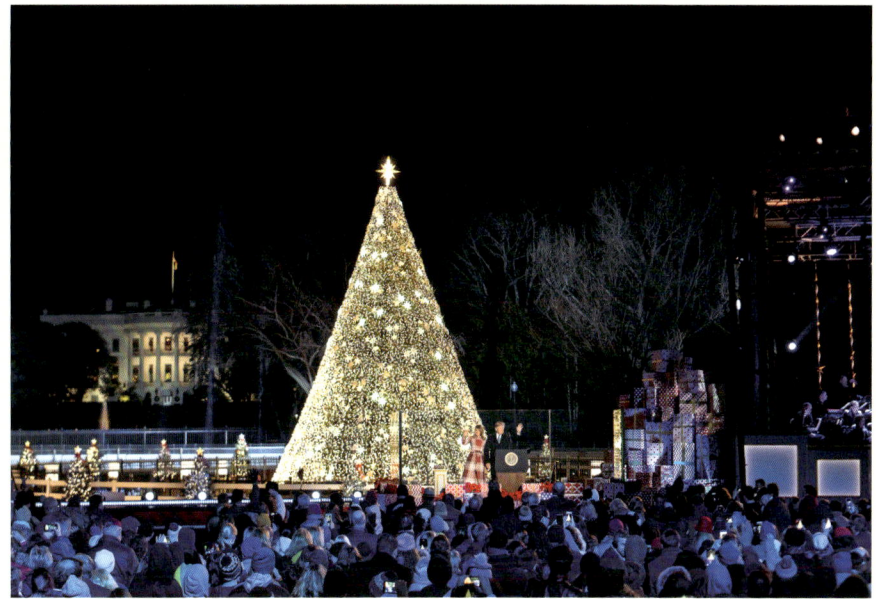

The tree is all lit up following the 97th annual National Christmas Tree Lighting Ceremony.

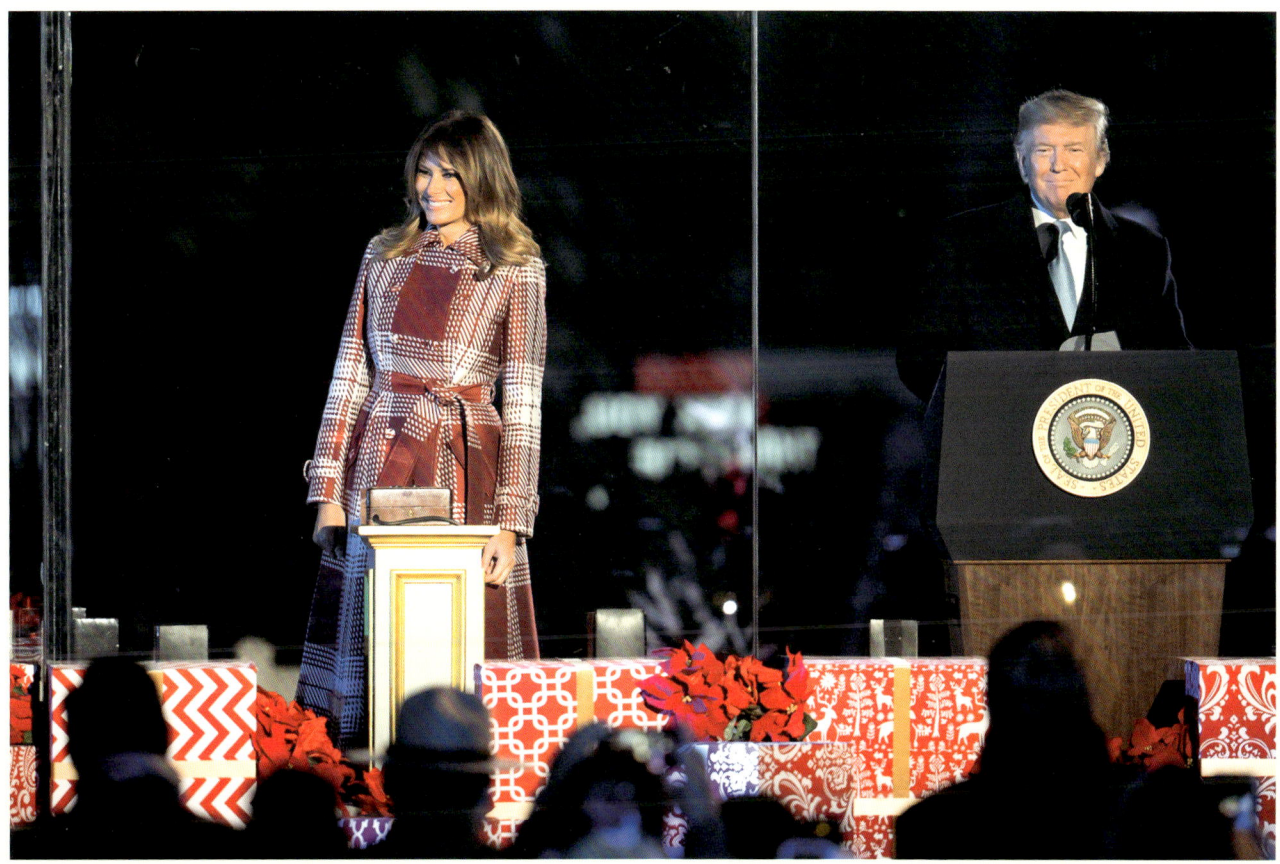

President Trump and the First Lady give their remarks at the 2019 National Christmas Tree Lighting Ceremony.

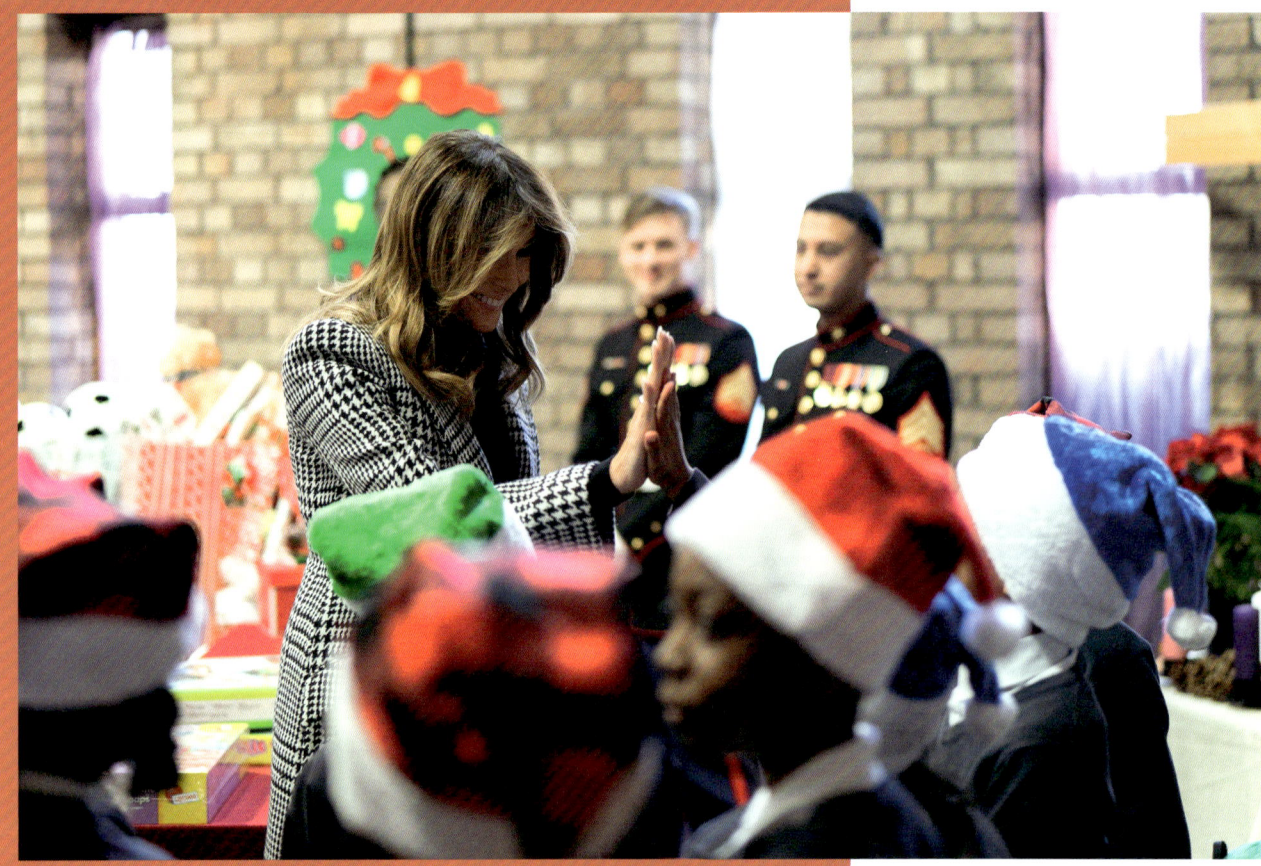

First Lady Melania Trump high fives a student from Baden Powell Primary School during a visit to the Salvation Army Clapton Center in London.

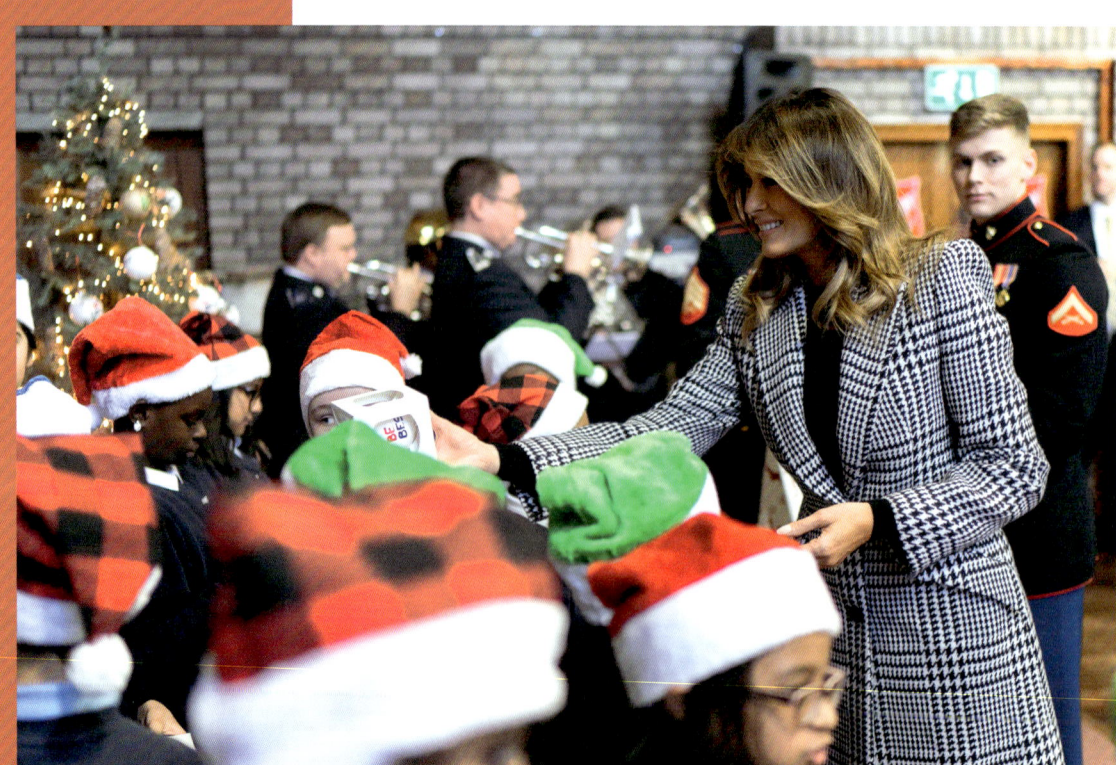

First Lady Melania Trump gives BE BEST Christmas ornaments to students from Baden Powell Primary School celebrating her official White House initiative which launched in 2018.

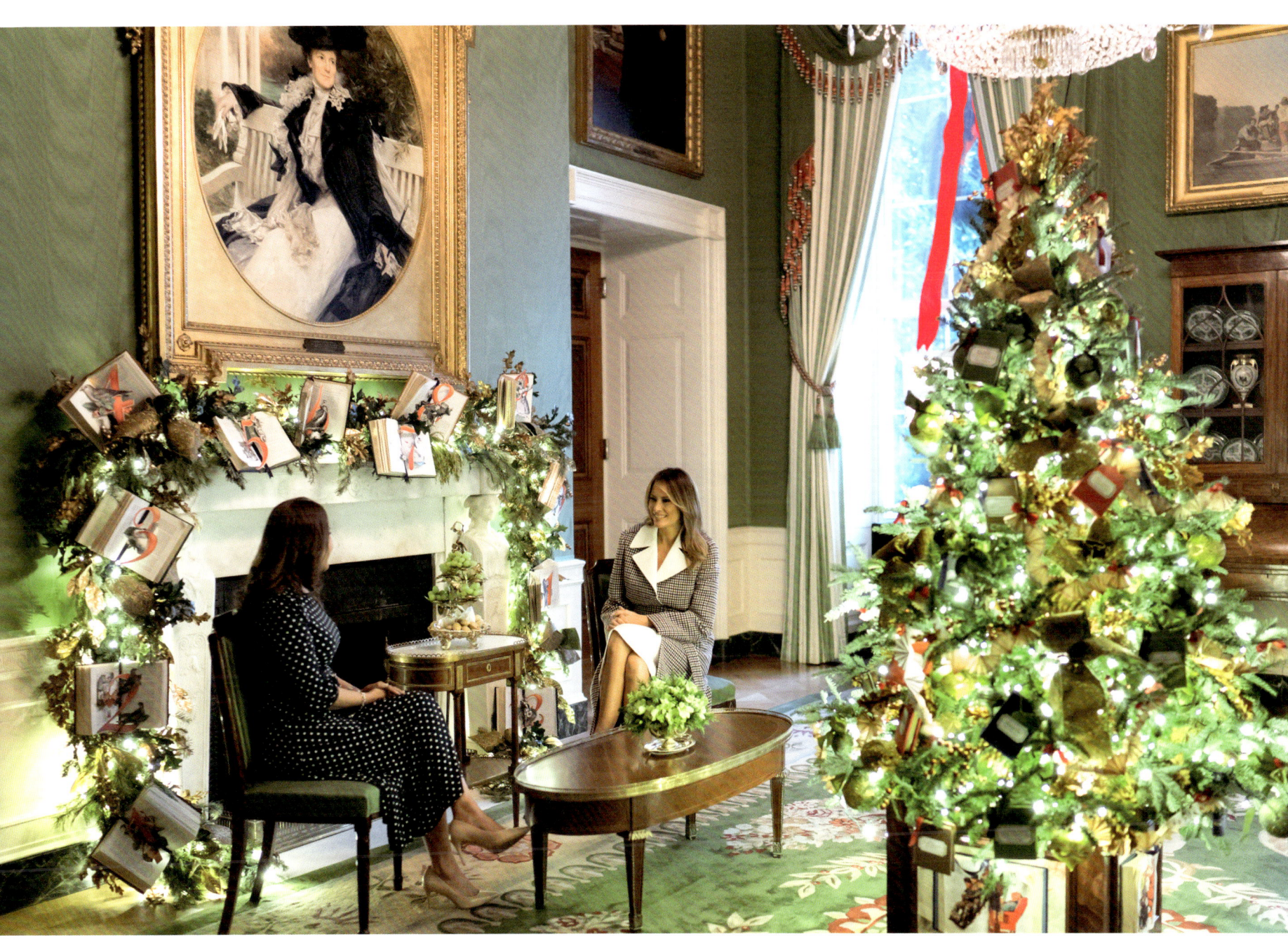

First Lady Melania Trump has tea with Mrs. Patricia Marroquin, wife of Guatemalan President Jimmy Morales, in the Green Room of the White House.

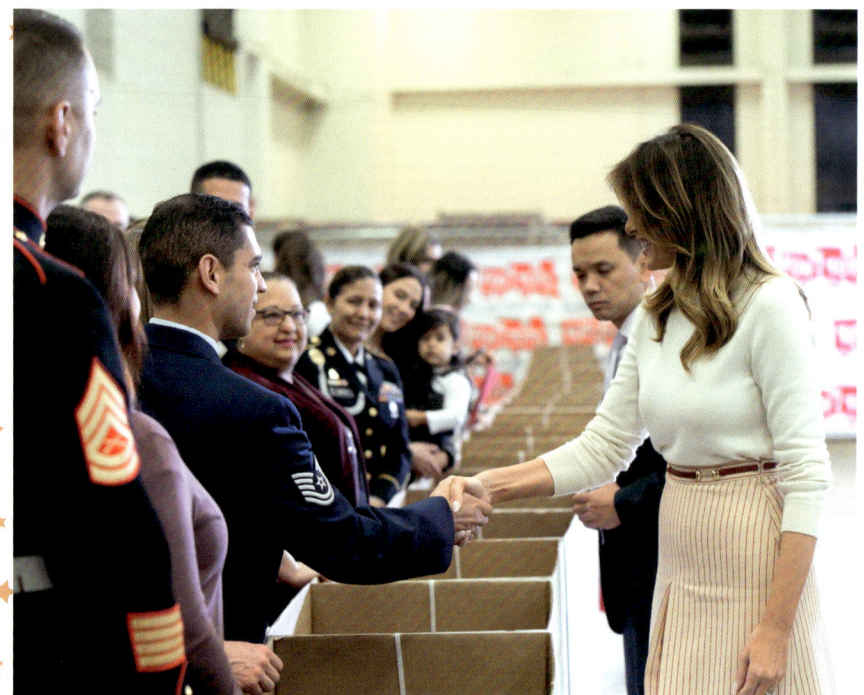

Mrs. Trump greets service members and their families attending a Toys for Tots Christmas Event at Joint Base Anacostia-Bolling in Washington, D.C.

First Lady Melania Trump writes Christmas cards to the troops with children attending a Toys for Tots Christmas Event at Joint Base Anacostia-Bolling in Washington, D.C.

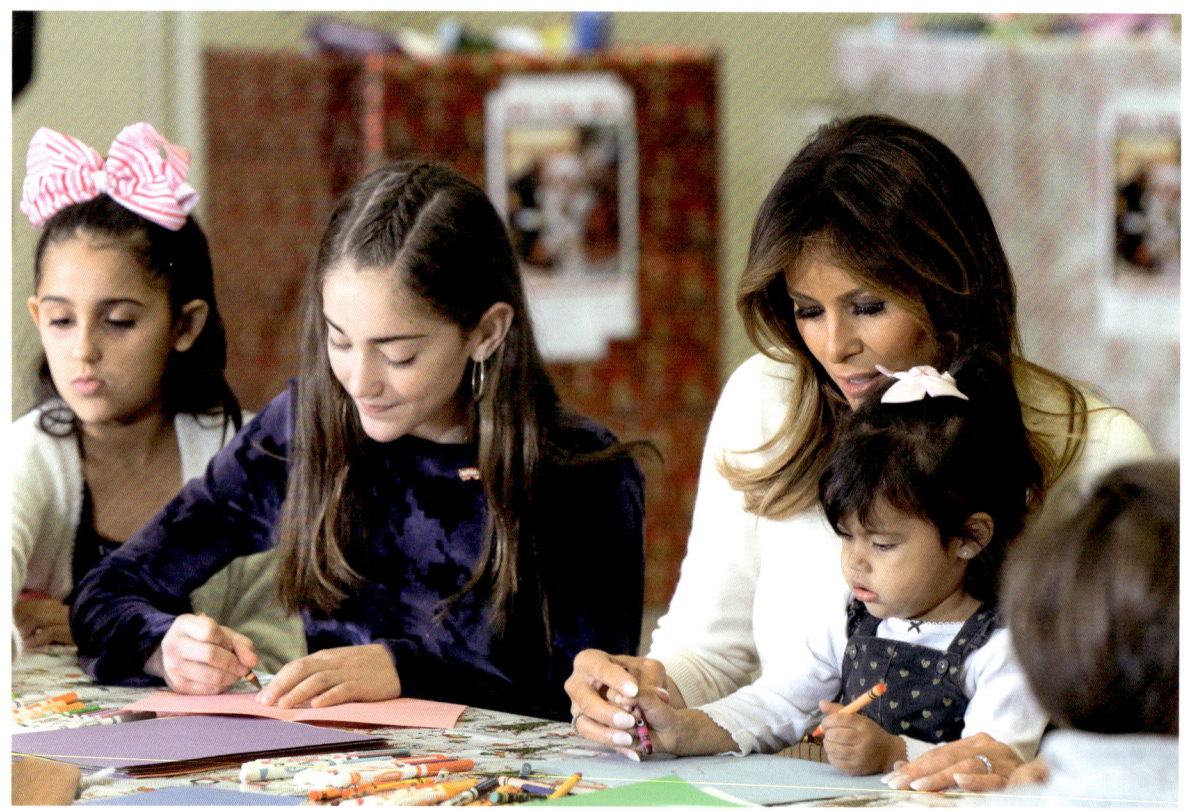

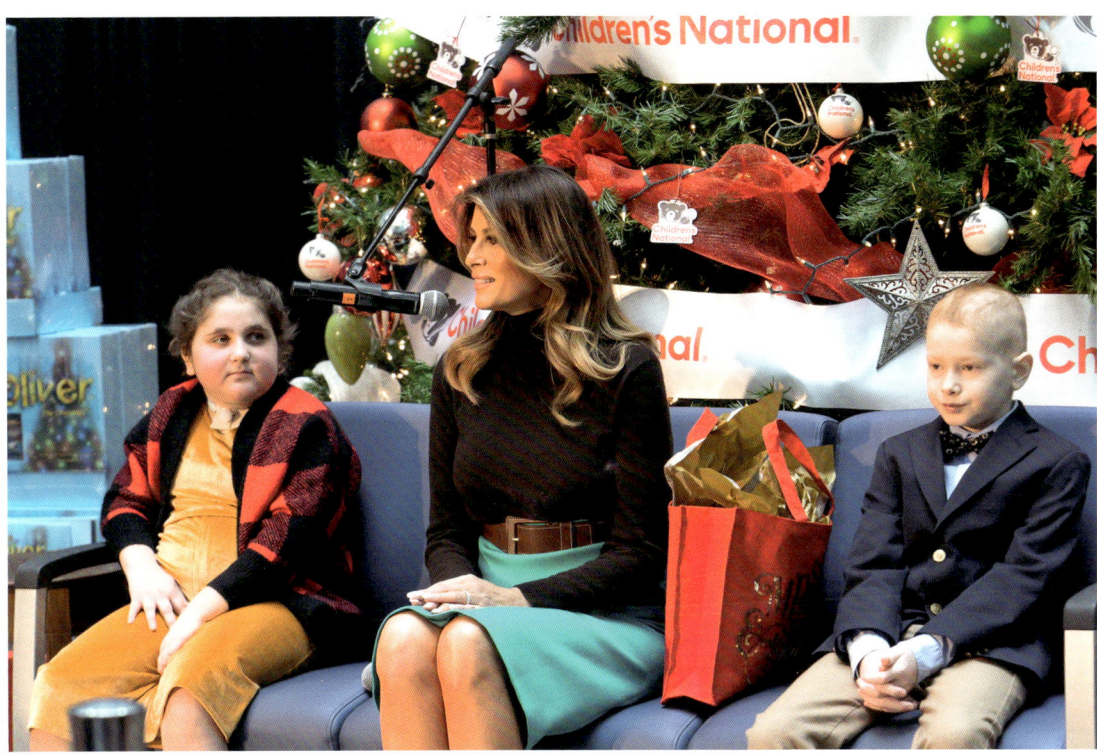

First Lady Melania Trump greets patients and families before reading *Oliver the Ornament Meets Belle* during a Christmas visit to Children's National Hospital.

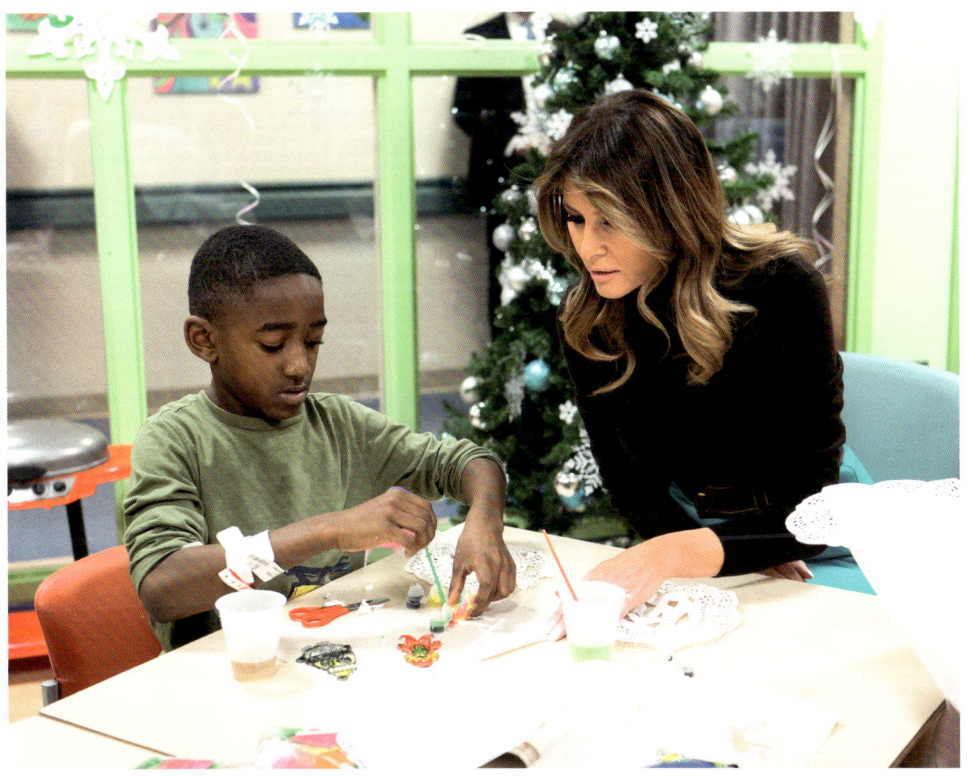

First Lady Melania Trump participates in holiday crafts with 8-year-old patient Dwayne Salmon during a Christmas visit to Children's National Hospital.

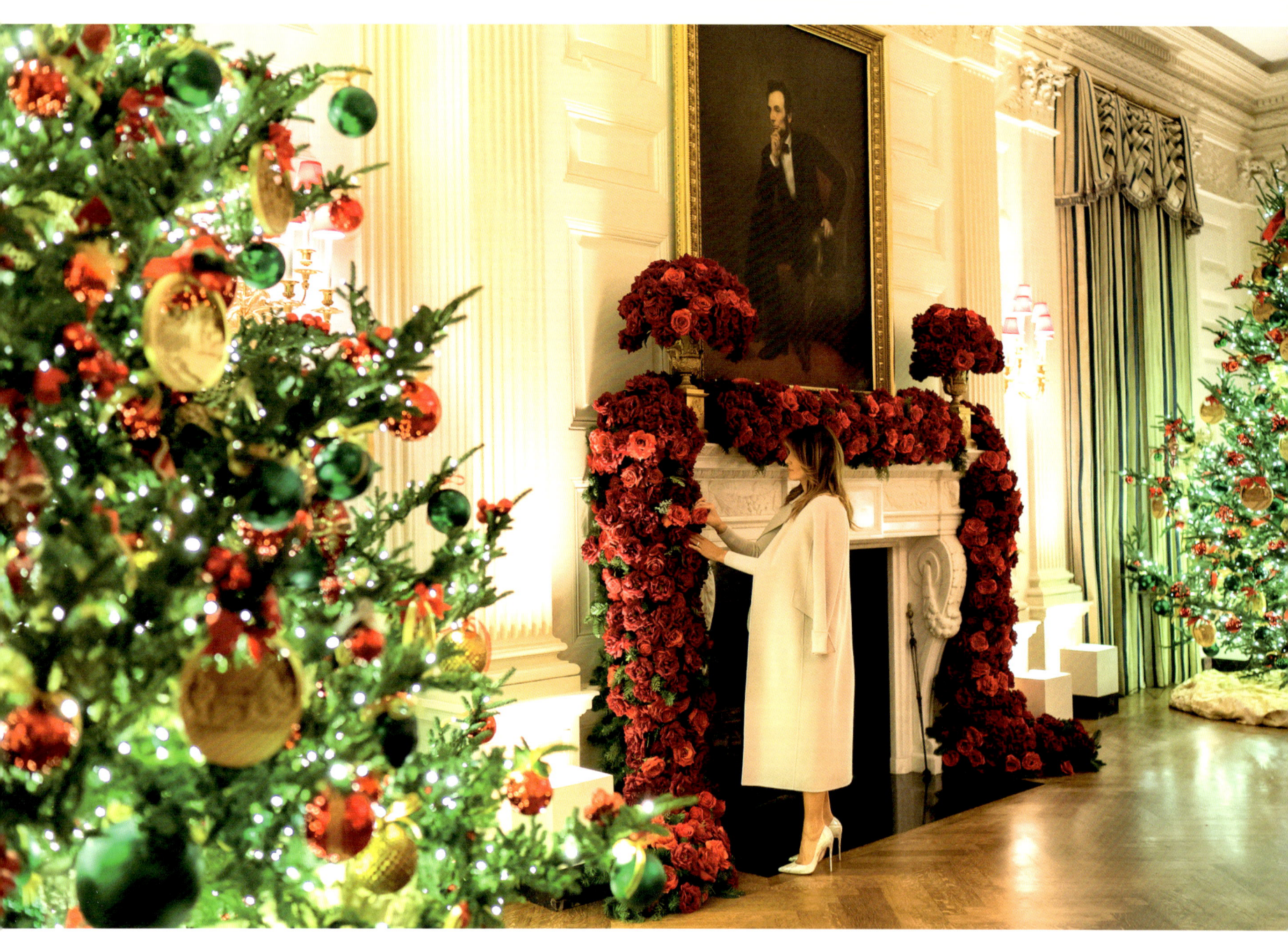

First Lady Melania Trump looks at a rose garland in the State Dining Room of the White House during a review of the Christmas decorations.

"This Christmas season I want to honor those who have shaped our country and made it the place we are proud to call home, and I am excited to announce our White House holiday theme, 'The Spirit of America.' When I travel the country, I am inspired by the hard working people and families that I meet. No matter which state they call home, many Americans share a strong set of values and appreciation for the traditions and history of our great nation. Thank you to all of the staff and volunteers who worked to make sure the People's House was ready for Christmas. Wishing everyone a very Merry Christmas and Happy New Year."

—First Lady Melania Trump, 2019

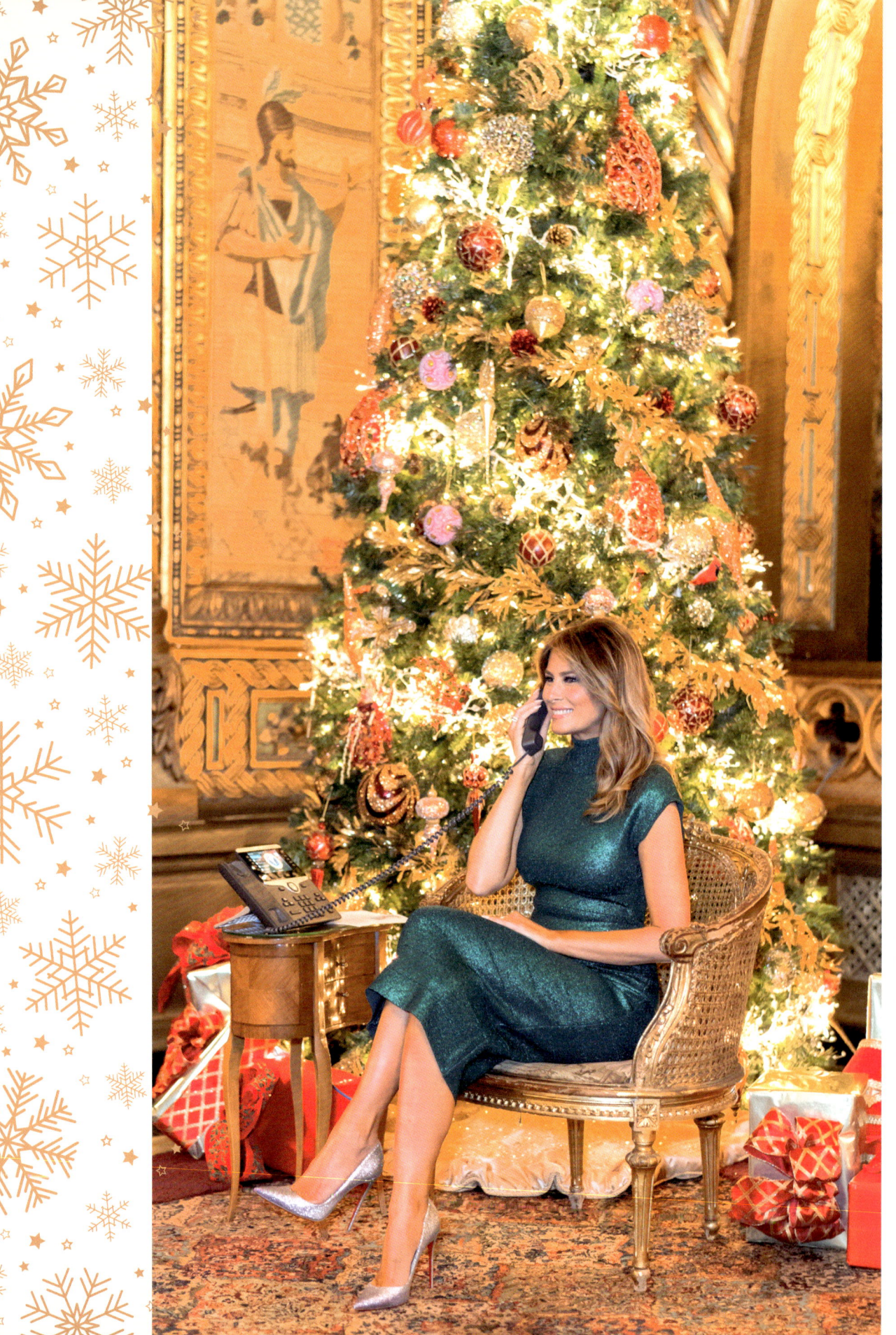

First Lady Melania Trump participates in NORAD Santa Tracker phone calls placed to children on Christmas Eve Tuesday, December 24, 2019, at Mar-a-Lago in Palm Beach, Florida. (Official White House Photo by Shealah Craighead)

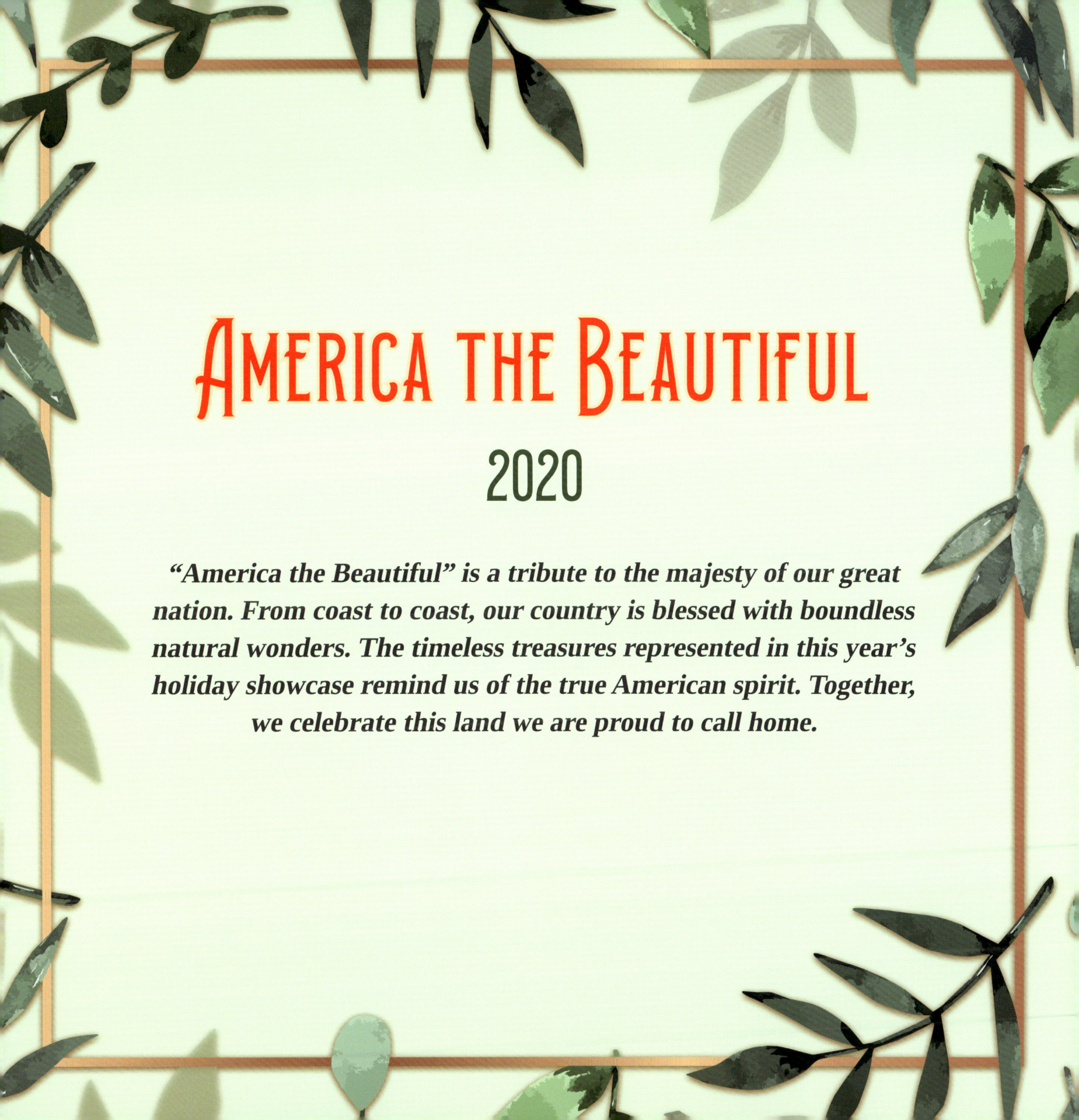

AMERICA THE BEAUTIFUL

2020

"America the Beautiful" is a tribute to the majesty of our great nation. From coast to coast, our country is blessed with boundless natural wonders. The timeless treasures represented in this year's holiday showcase remind us of the true American spirit. Together, we celebrate this land we are proud to call home.

The East Colonnade celebrated the diverse landscapes found across the United States. Arranged by region, classical urns held foliage representative of the official tree of each state and territory. The East Garden Room showcased holiday cards sent by first families throughout the past twelve administrations. The Vermeil Room featured over 1,600 decorations, inspired by First Lady Jacqueline Kennedy's "People's House," the living museum of the White House. President John F. Kennedy's portrait is featured on each of the graceful trees.

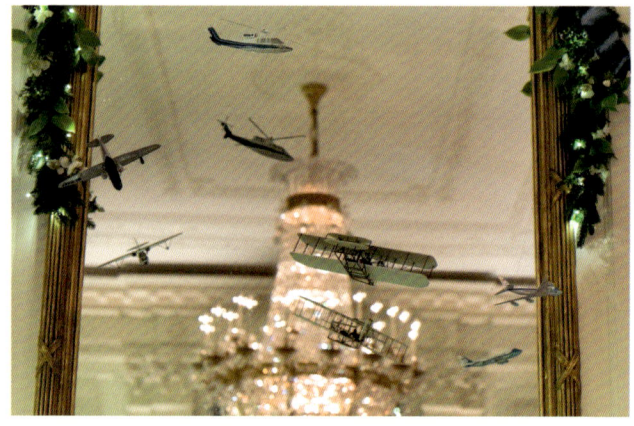

The mirrors of the East Room of the White House are decorated with planes and helicopters, celebrating American innovation in transportation.

The library shone a spotlight on the 19th Amendment, which granted women the right to vote in 1920, by celebrating the women who were pioneers for gender equality and the impact they had on the history of the United States. The decorations honored the women on the cutting edge of American achievement and how they paved the way for women today. The China Room was set with a home scene of timeless traditions and delicious candies and cookies. Christmas stockings for the First Family hung from the fireplace.

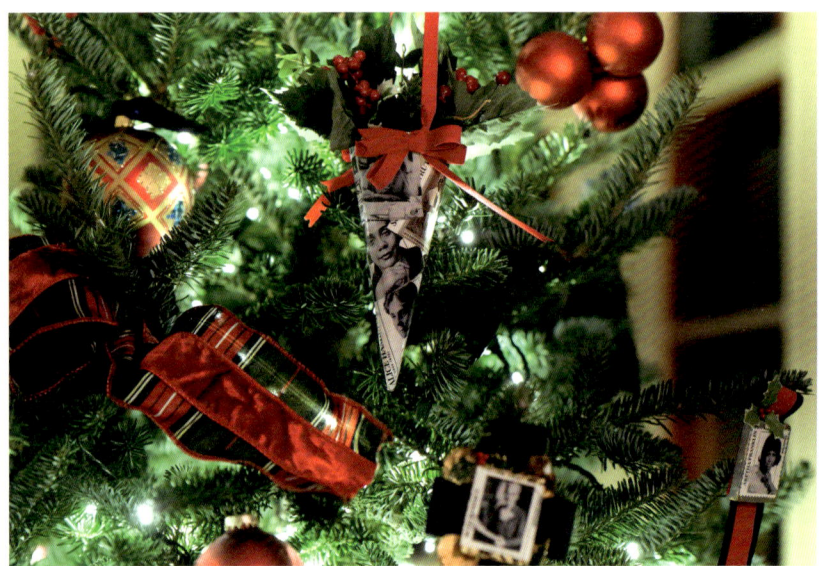

Images of historic female American leaders and artists decorate the Christmas trees in the Vermeil Room of the White House.

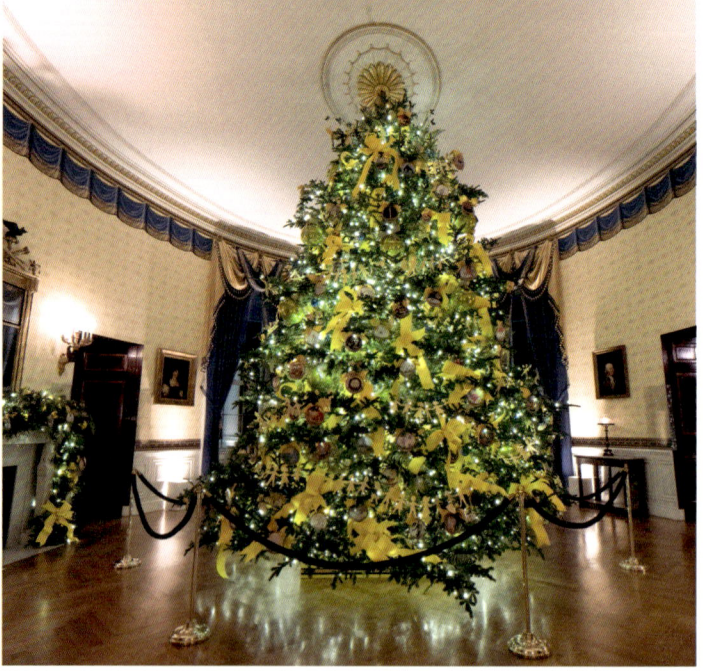

The 2020 White House Christmas Tree is decorated with the artwork of children from around the country, who were asked to depict what made their state special.

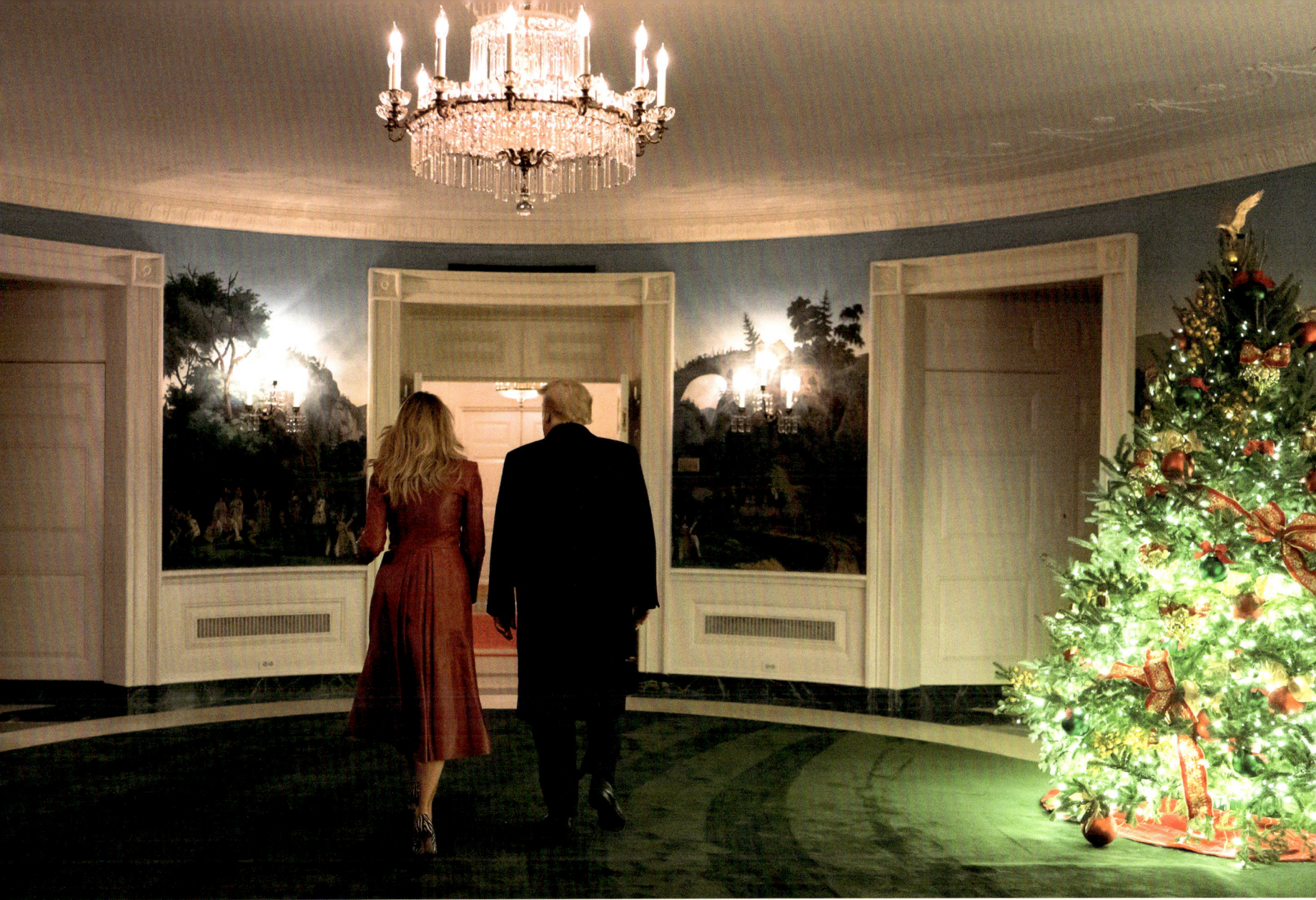

Even the Diplomatic Reception Room of the White House is decorated for the Christmas season! (Official White House Photo by Tia Dufour)

Up in the East Room, the decorations represented "America on the Move," with planes, trains, and automobiles. From the railroad to the moon landing, nothing shines in the history of the United States quite like the innovation and technology of travel—whether on land, sea, air, or the boundless frontiers of space.

The Blue Room was lit up by the official White House Christmas tree, a gorgeous Fraser fir representing the splendor of our country through the unique perspective of America's children. Students from California to Virginia were asked to artistically depict what makes their state beautiful. This artwork was placed on the branches of the tree, which was decked out in rays of yellow and gold to represent children in First Lady Melania Trump's Be Best Initiative.

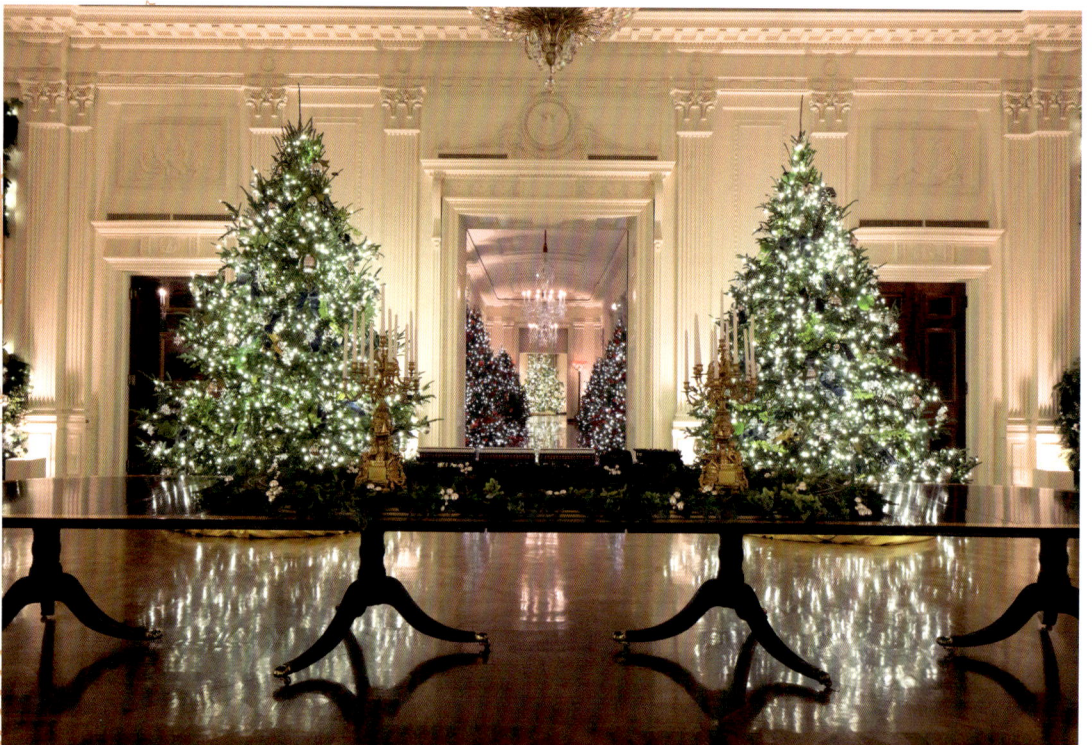

The White House Express train decorates the center table of the East Room of the White House. The East Room is dedicated to innovation in travel, featuring planes, trains, and automobiles to show America's great history of expansion and travel.

The Green Room decorations celebrate the beauty of American wildlife and the diversity of our landscape, with butterflies and birds abundant on the trees and mantles.

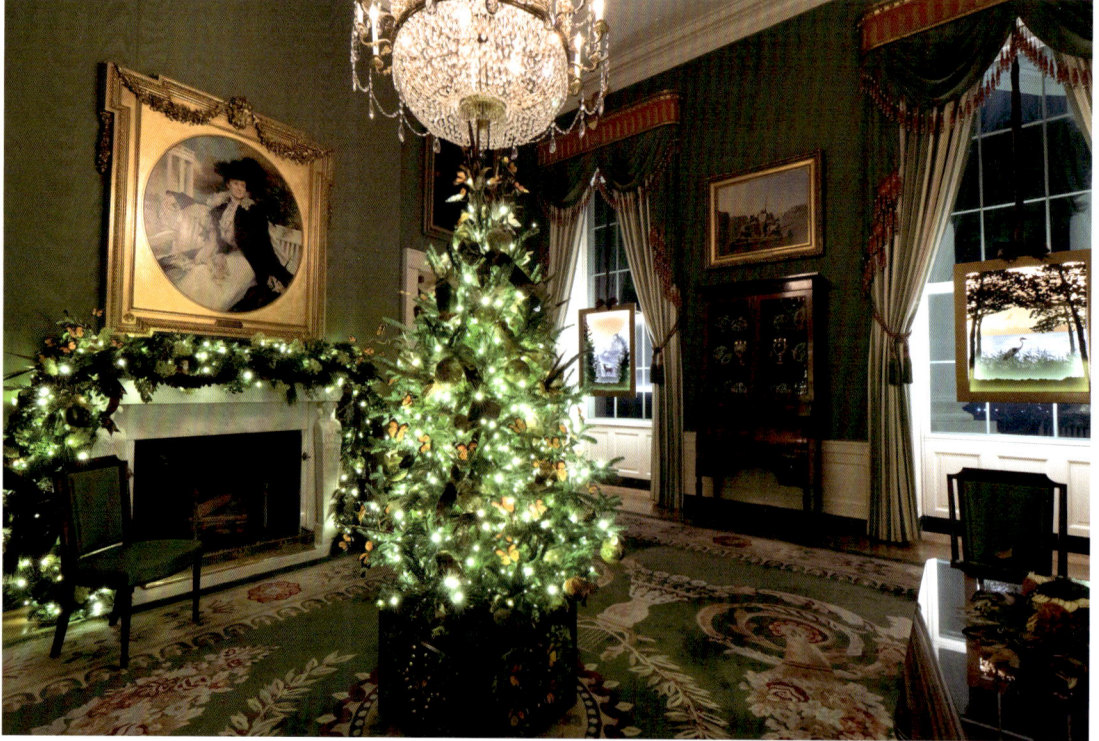

Right: First Lady Melania Trump reviews the Christmas decorations in the Cross Hall of the White House, meant to represent the many gifts of the holiday season.

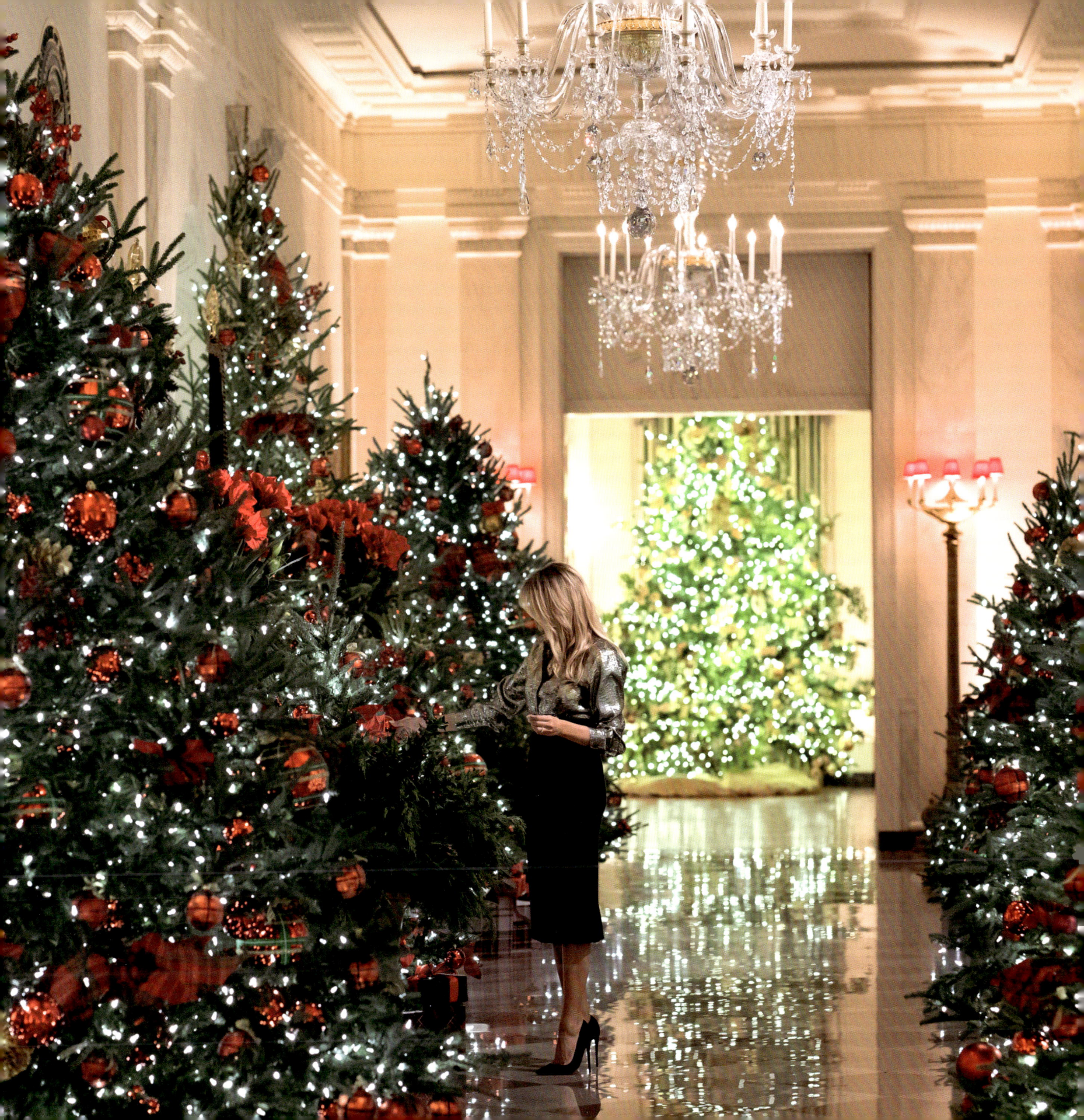

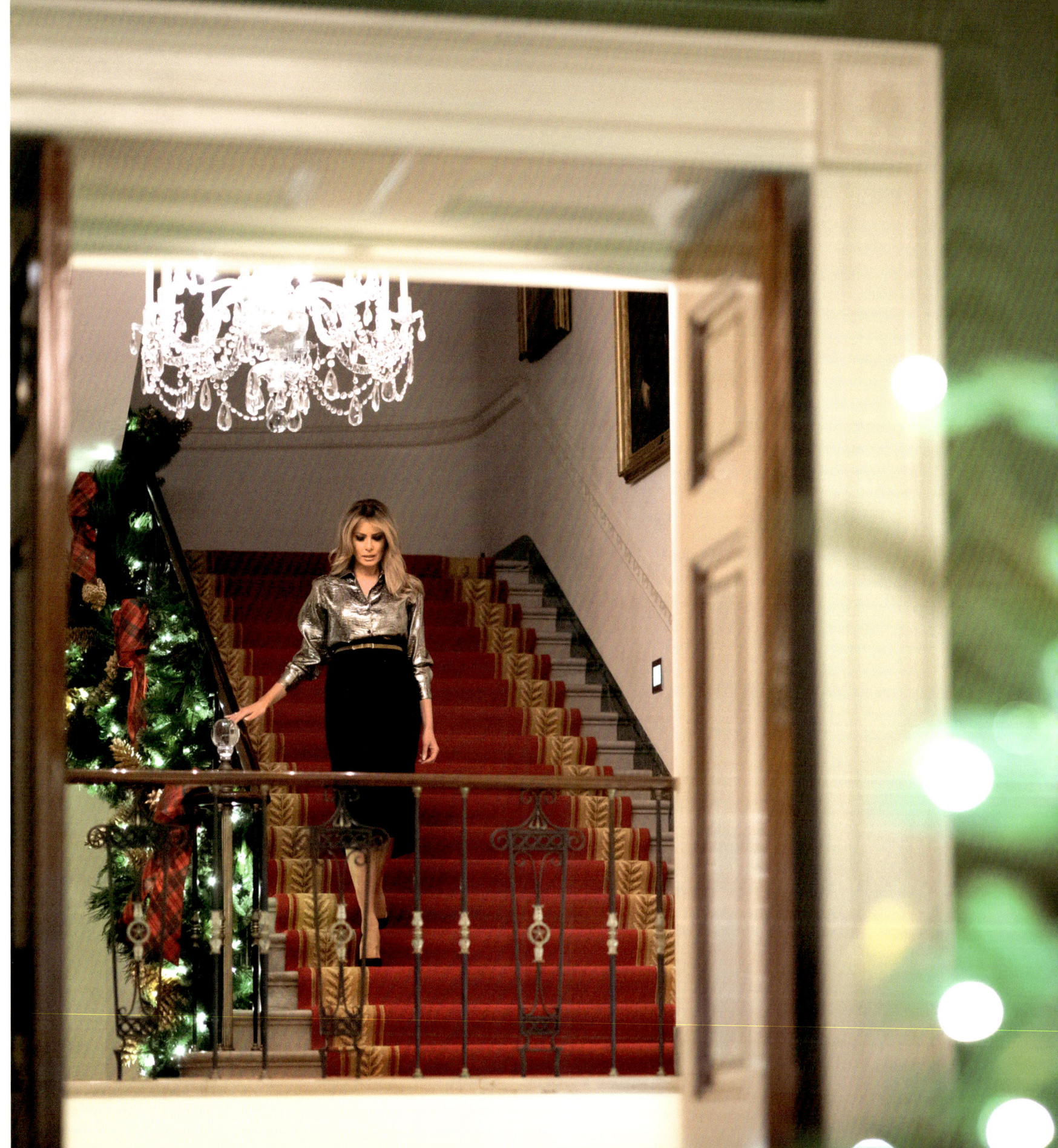

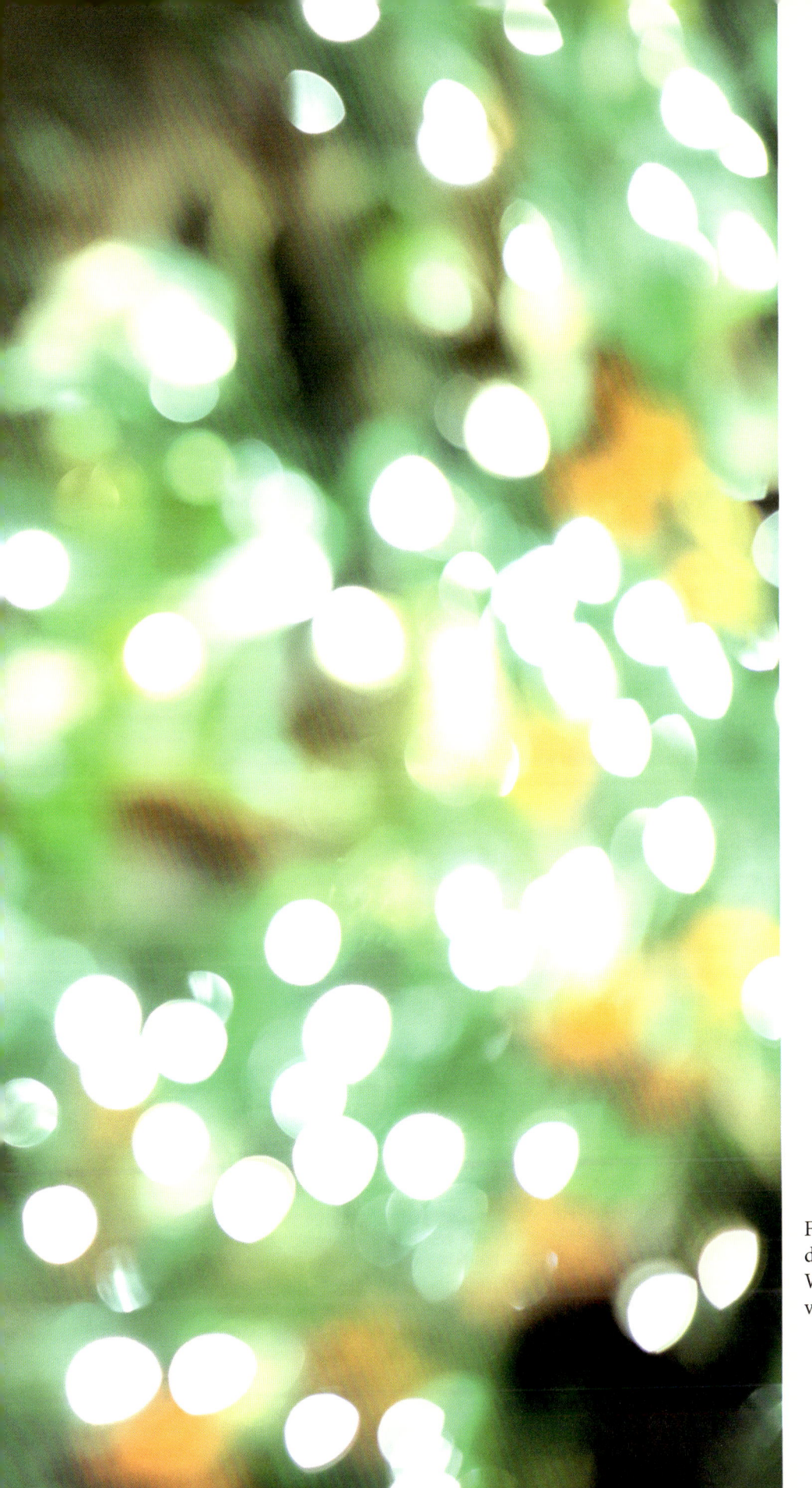

First Lady Melania Trump walks down the Grand Staircase of the White House as she arrives to review the Christmas decorations.

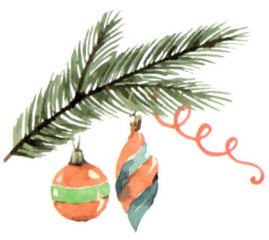

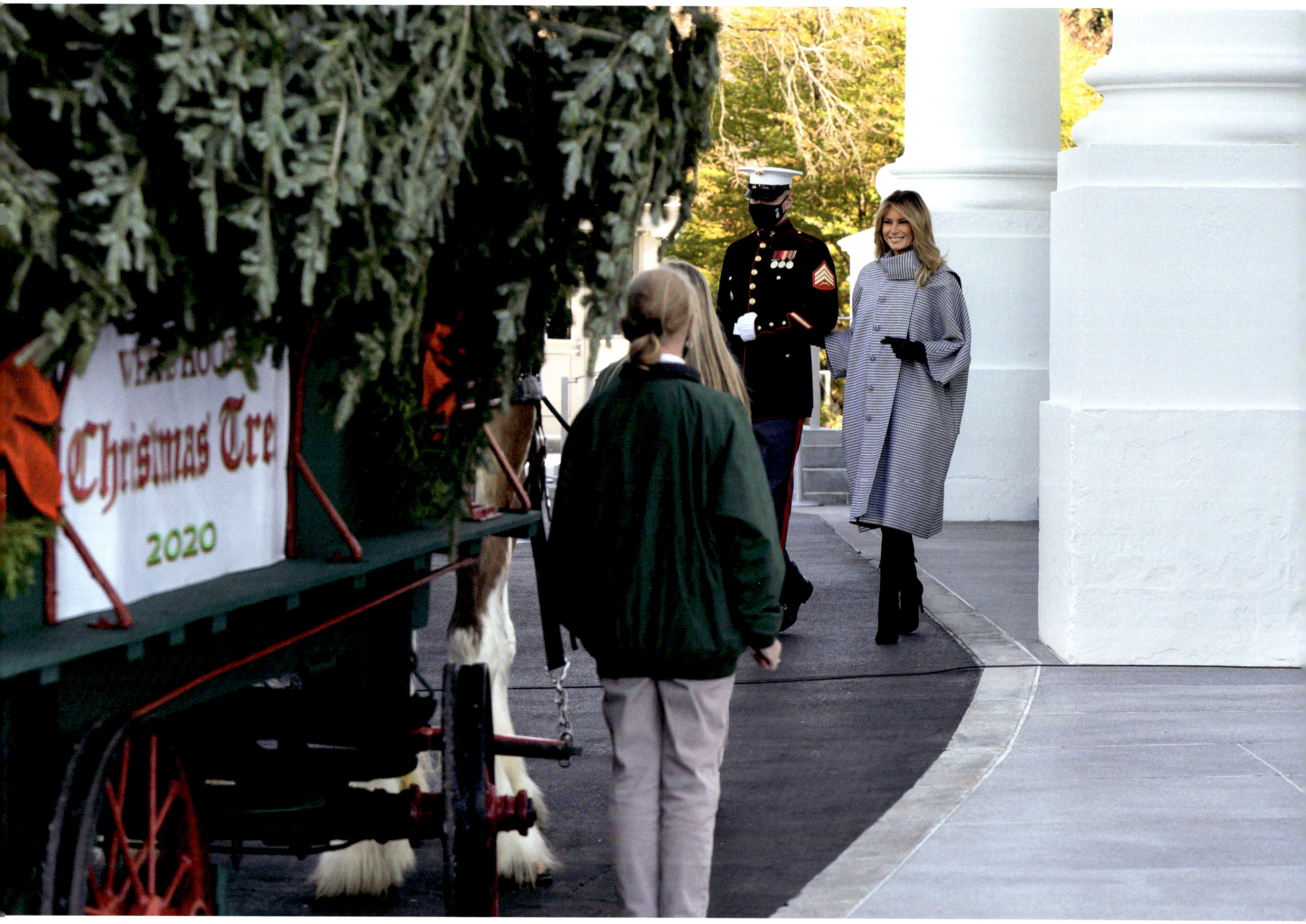

First Lady Melania Trump arrives to receive the White House Christmas Tree at the North Portico of the White House.
The tree this year is an 18.5-foot Fraser Fir from Shepherdstown, West Virginia.

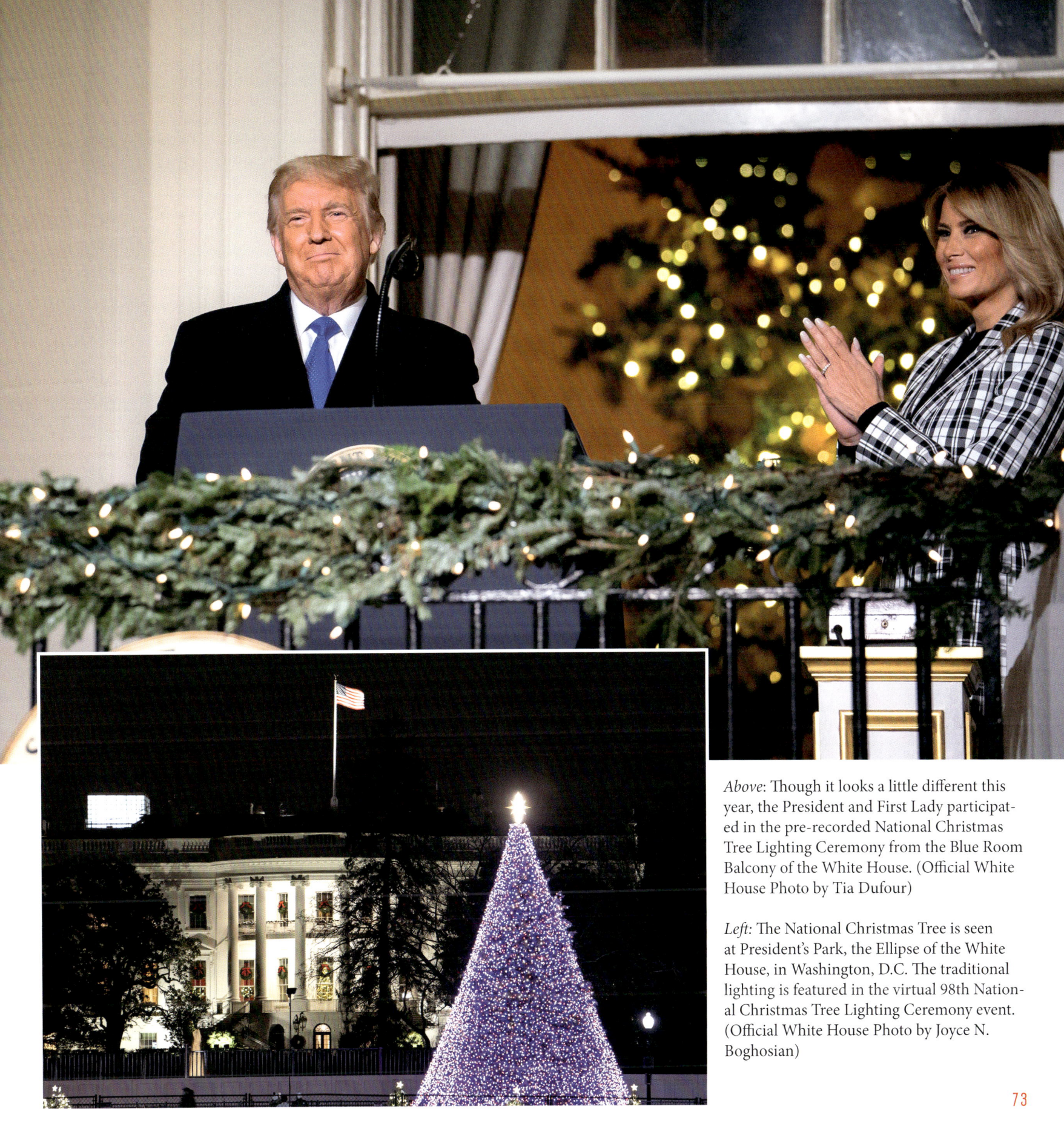

Above: Though it looks a little different this year, the President and First Lady participated in the pre-recorded National Christmas Tree Lighting Ceremony from the Blue Room Balcony of the White House. (Official White House Photo by Tia Dufour)

Left: The National Christmas Tree is seen at President's Park, the Ellipse of the White House, in Washington, D.C. The traditional lighting is featured in the virtual 98th National Christmas Tree Lighting Ceremony event. (Official White House Photo by Joyce N. Boghosian)

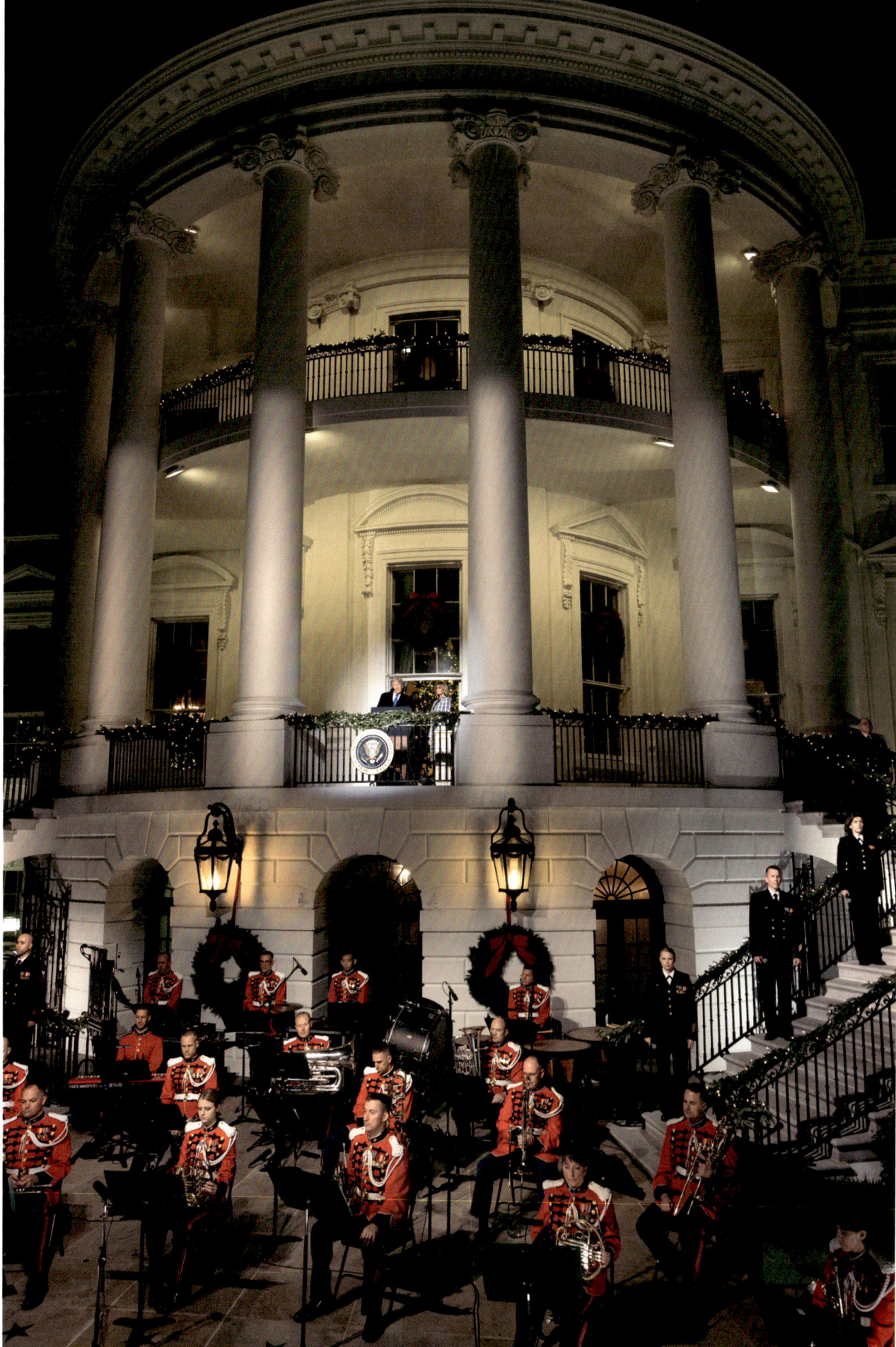

A wide angle shot of the President and First Lady delivering remarks during the pre-recorded National Christmas Tree Lighting Ceremony.

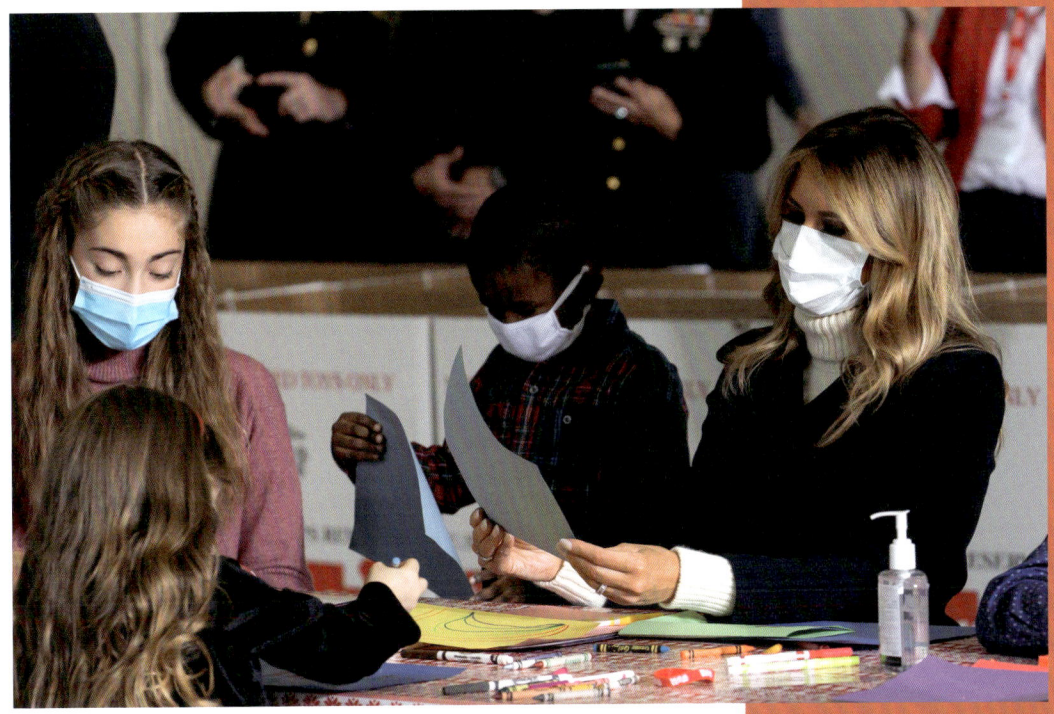

First Lady Melania Trump talks with children writing Christmas cards to the troops during a Toys for Tots Christmas event.

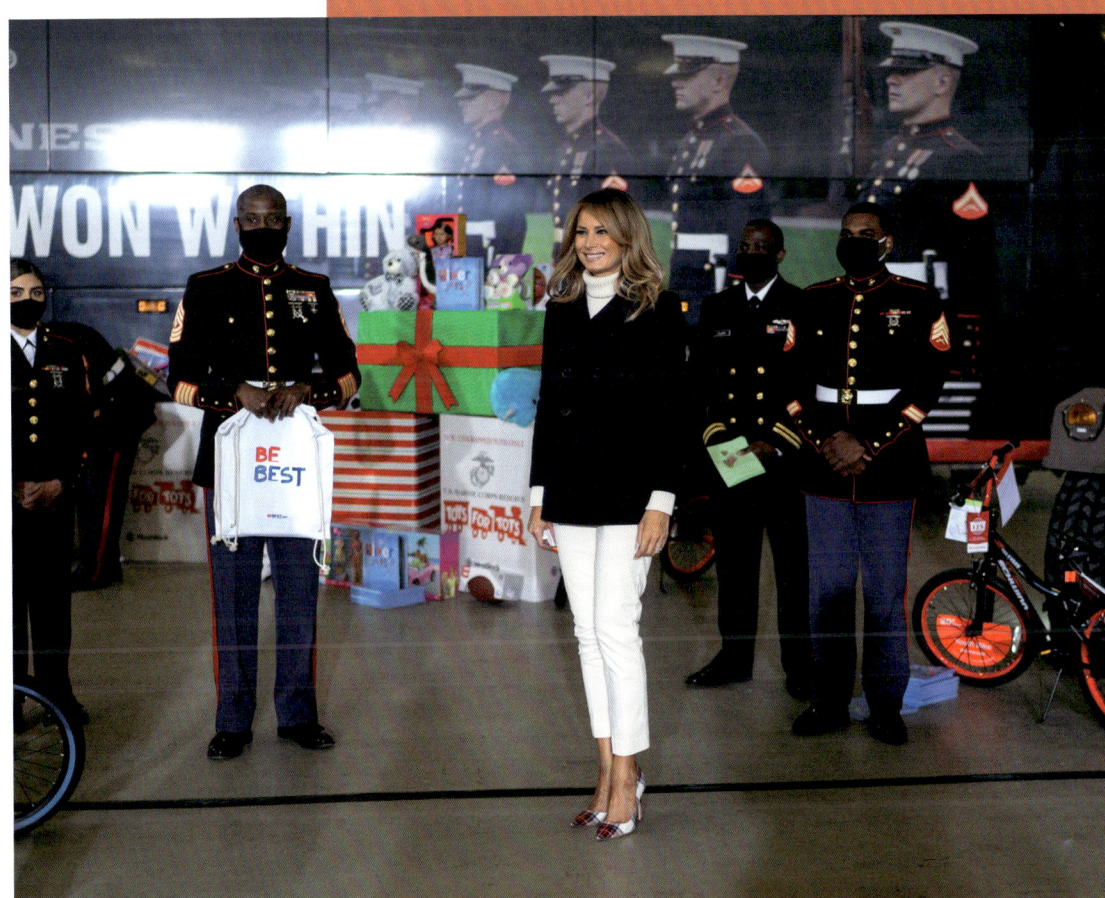

First Lady Melania Trump, joined by members of the United States Marines, greets children participating in a Toys for Tots Christmas event at Joint Base Anacostia-Bolling in Washington, D.C.

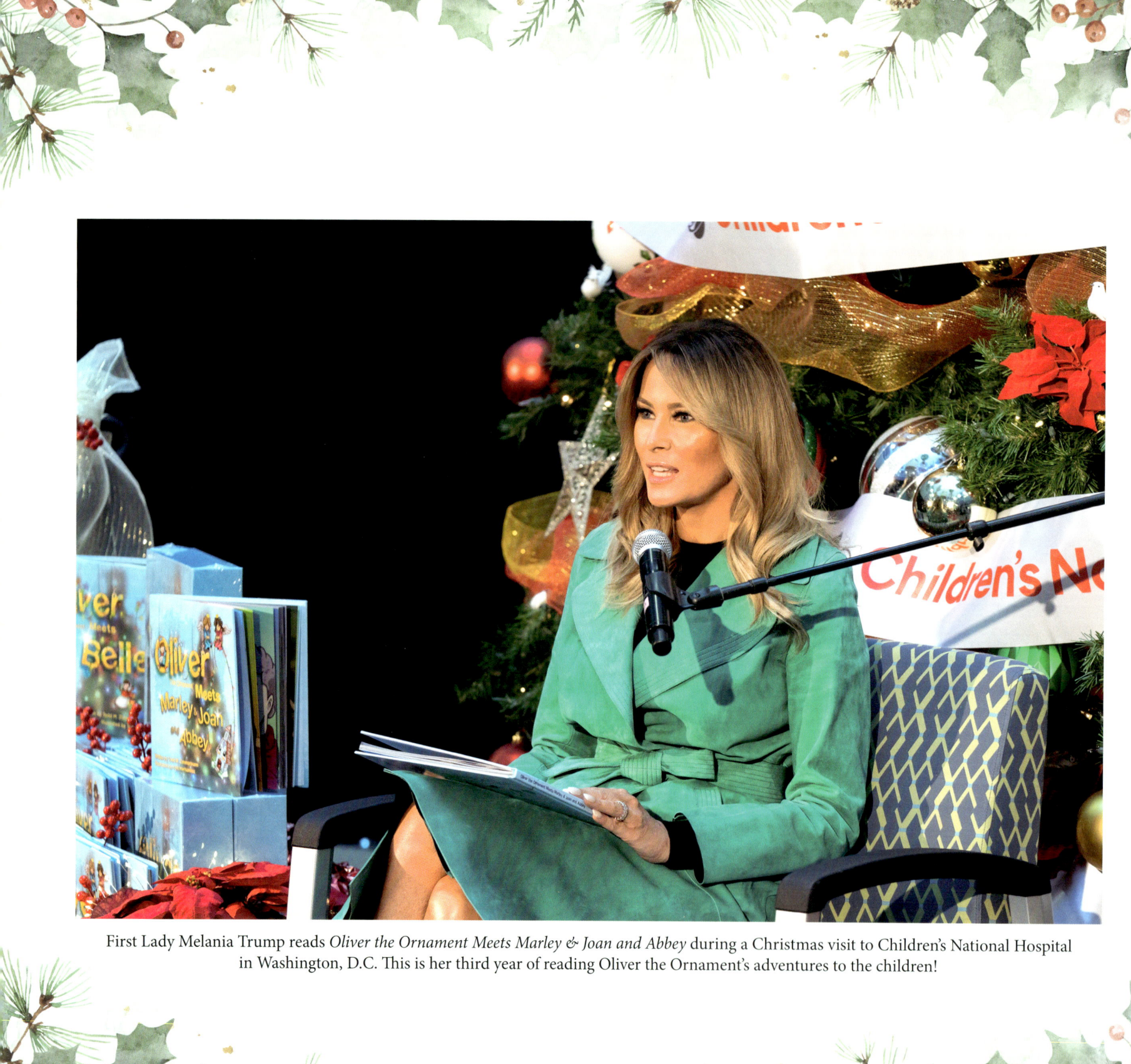

First Lady Melania Trump reads *Oliver the Ornament Meets Marley & Joan and Abbey* during a Christmas visit to Children's National Hospital in Washington, D.C. This is her third year of reading Oliver the Ornament's adventures to the children!

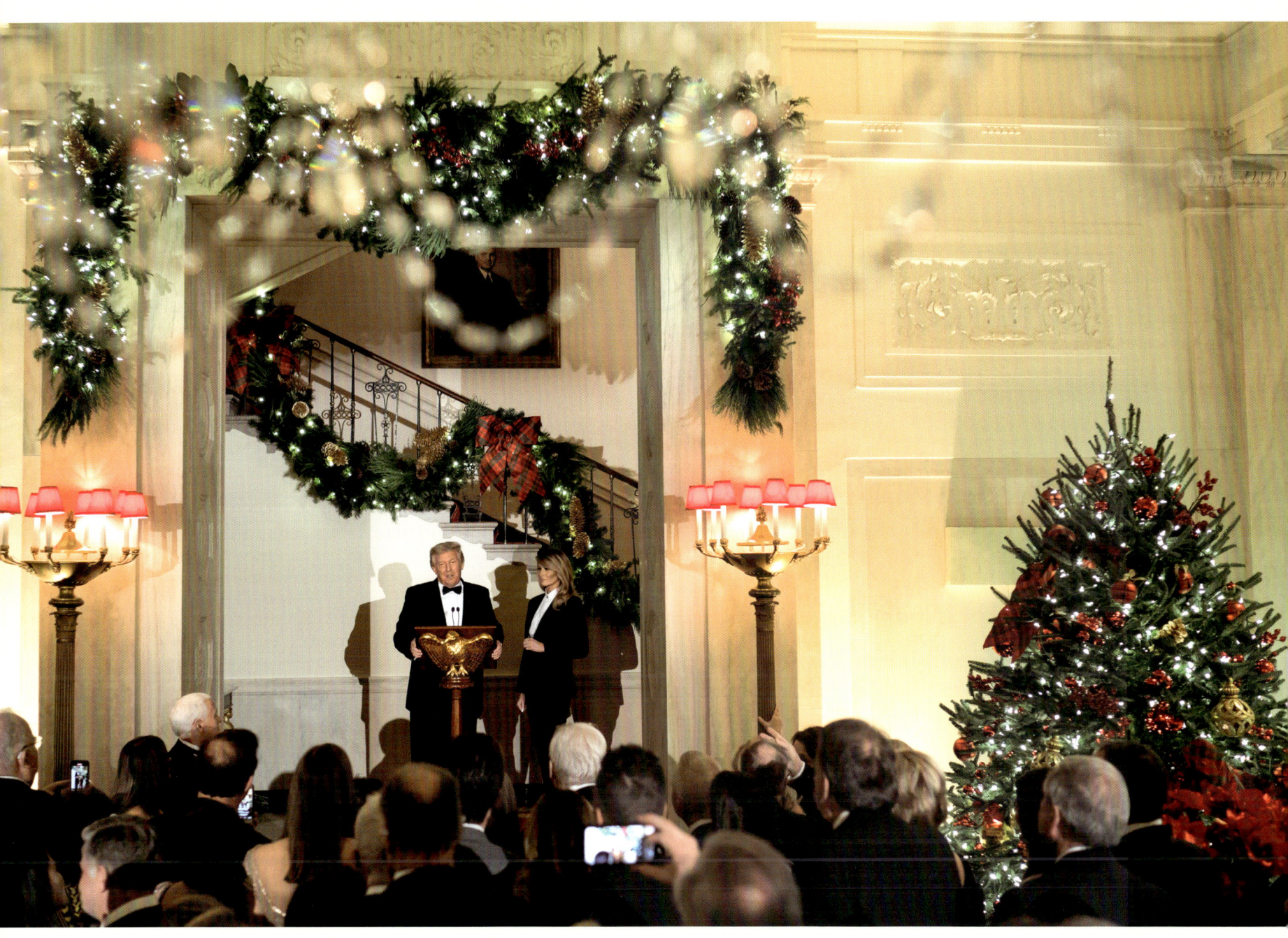

The First Lady and the President deliver remarks during the Congressional Ball Thursday, December 10, 2020, in the Grand Foyer of the White House.

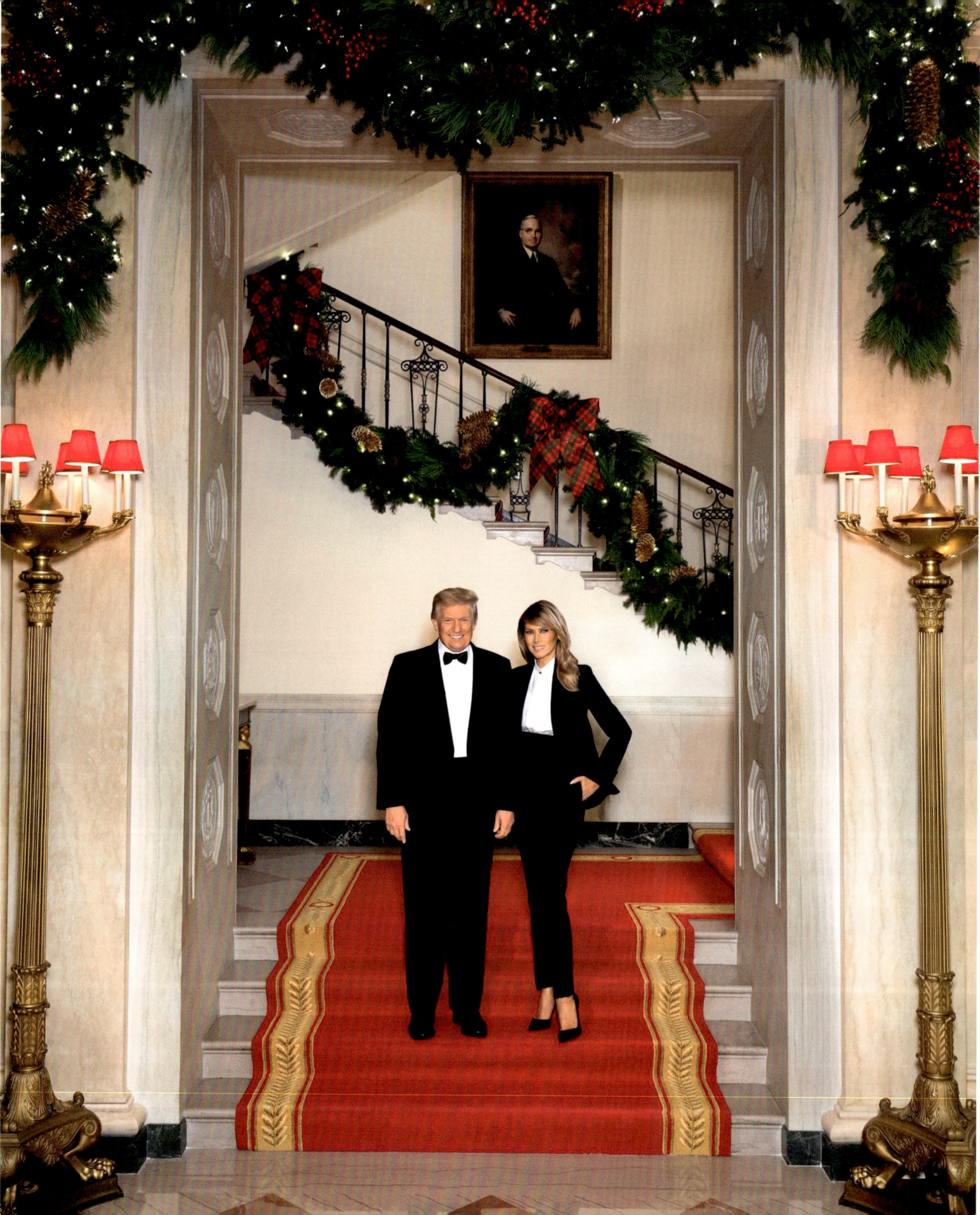

"The First Lady and I send our warmest wishes to all Americans as we celebrate Christmas. While our gatherings might look different than in years past, this Christmas, like every Christmas, is an opportunity for us to celebrate the birth of our Savior, Jesus Christ, and show our heartfelt gratitude for the abundant blessings God has bestowed upon our lives and country.

"In this season of peace, we cherish the warmth, generosity, and faith that breathe life into our holiday gatherings. The love we share with our family and friends fills our hearts with joy, just ast the story of Christ's birth inspires people all over the world. This year we come together as proud Americans–grateful for our sacred right to worship freely and to openly profess our trust in the enduring light and promise of the coming of God.

"To military families who are unable to celebrate Christmas together this year, our nation humbly thanks you for your service and sacrifice. We are forever indebted to those who courageously serve our country in uniform–and those who walk alongside them. We also thank our Nation's first responders, law enforcement officers, and frontline medical professionals who work tirelessly to serve and protect our communities. Your daily contributions are an example of the selfless love of God and remind us of the noble principles we strive to live by, especially during this special time of year.

"To all Americans, and to all our friends around the globe celebrating today, we wish you a very Merry Christmas and a peaceful and prosperous New Year."

—President Donald J. Trump, 2020

President Trump and First Lady Melania Trump in their official 2020 Christmas portrait, on the Grand staircase of the White House.

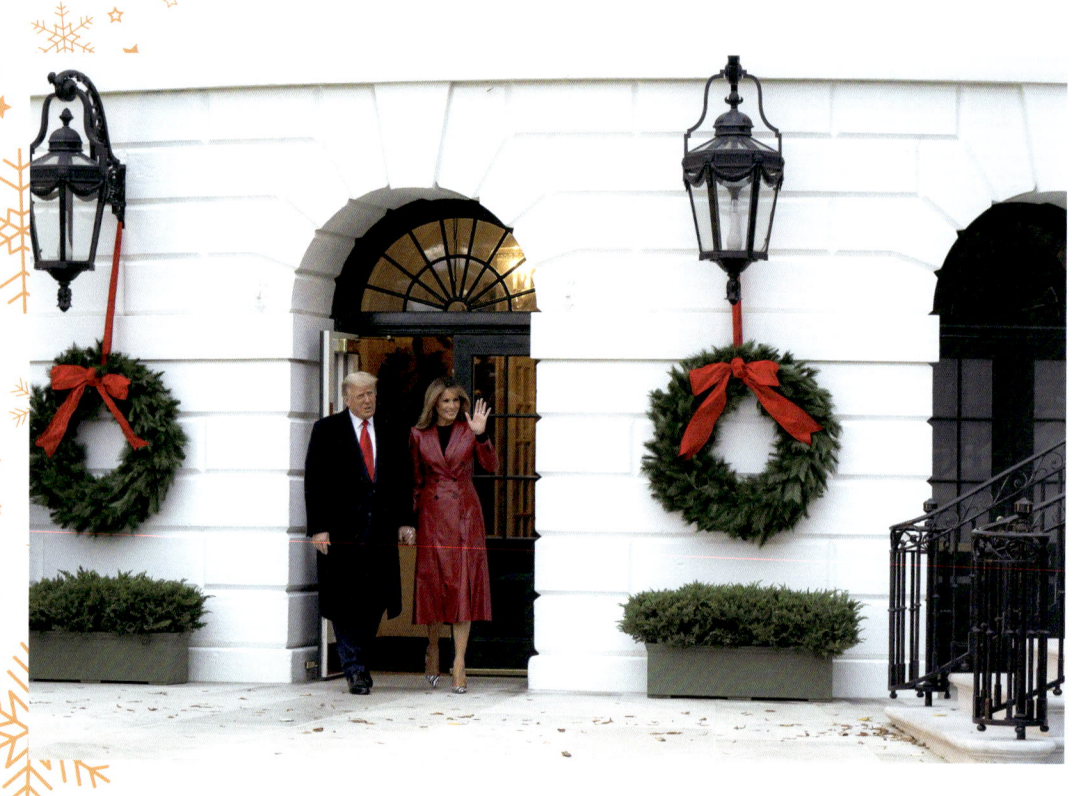

President Donald J. Trump and First Lady Melania Trump wave to guests and members of the press as they depart the South Portico. (Official White House Photo by Tia Dufour)

President Trump speaks with military service personnel on duty around the world December 25, 2020, during a Christmas Day video call at Mar-a-Lago in Palm Beach, Florida. (Official White House Photo by Shealah Craighead)

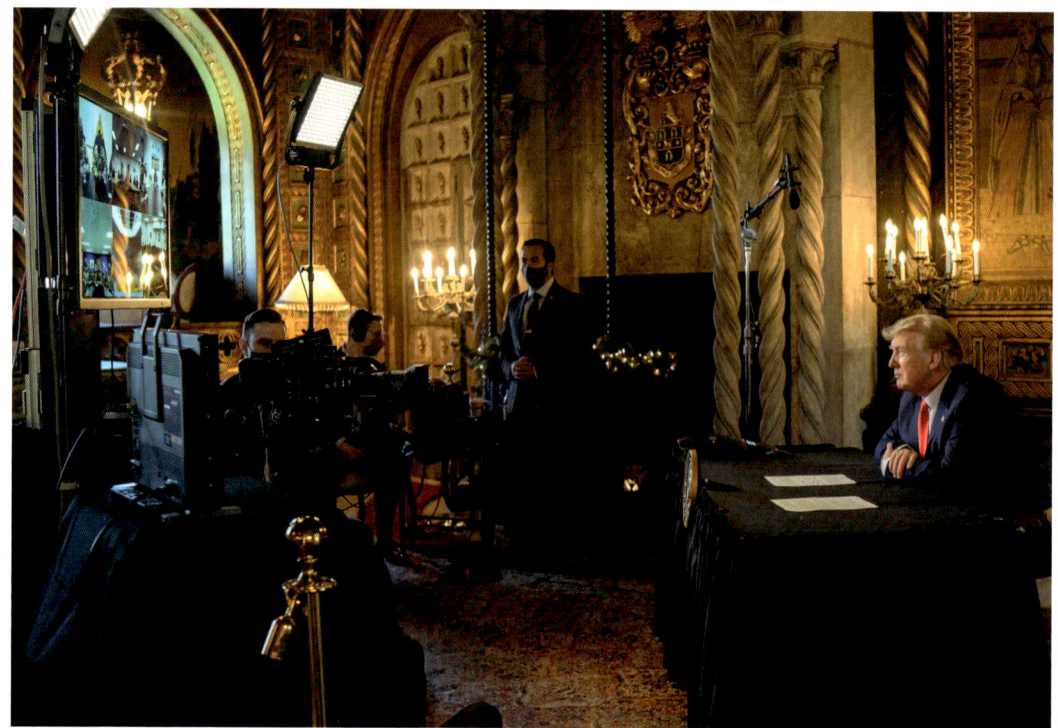